WORKING OUT OF DOORS
WITH YOUNG PEOPLE

Written, designed and illustrated by Alan Smith

Published by the ITRC 19 Elmbank Street, Glasgow G2 4PB

Published by the ITRC 19 Elmbank Street, Glasgow G2 4PB
© Alan Smith 1987.

2nd Printing 1989

Printed in Great Britain by
Bell & Bain Ltd, Glasgow

ISBN 1 85202 002 4

CONTENTS

ACKNOWLEDGEMENTS

In all stages of writing this book I have received help and support from numerous sources.

I would particularly like to thank my two colleagues Geoff Lloyd and Dave Batty for their enthusiastic help which has often involved the trying out and testing of my ideas.

As part of the 'Project in Alternative Curriculum Experiences' (PACE), extra time and funds have been available for Outdoor Education which has given me the opportunity to develop many of the exercises. I would like to acknowledge the support of Nottinghamshire County Council in this respect.

Special credit must be given to my students who over a number of years, have unwittingly proved the value of working out of doors'.

Alan Dearling (previously Publications Officer for the Scottish I.T. Resource Centre) has given me valuable support and advice throughout the early stages of this book, without which the book would have taken much longer to produce. I would also like to acknowledge Alan Dearling for some of my initial inspiration generated by three books which he has edited, 'The Youth Games Book', 'The Youth Arts and Craft Book', and 'The Small Group Holiday Guide'.

Stuart Collins, my companion on numerous outdoor expeditions, has done a marvellous job of finding hundreds of mistakes in the original pages of this book. His knowledgable advice on the orienteering chapter has been especially valuable.

I am grateful to everyone else who has contributed their support, guidance and their criticism in order to help me complete this book.

INTRODUCTION

The contents of this book represent a selection of successful activities and games, developed over many years of teaching in a variety of outdoor situations. Hopefully they will make a useful contribution to the work of leaders and teachers engaged in outdoor education. With some optimism I would like to think that those who have not already been bitten by the outdoor bug, will be tempted to try out some of these ideas.

Leaders expecting to find a book full of ready made lesson plans, will be disappointed, since the pages have been designed to give <u>basic</u> ideas for exercises and games. Most leaders and teachers will need to adapt or modify these ideas to fit their situation, and will need to consider the experience of their students, the resources available, and the outdoor conditions.

By careful selection, the ideas contained in the six chapters could be included in a planned programme for: a residential week, a training course lasting several weeks, or a 'one off' day trip, but some attention to the appropriate sequence and variety of activities would be necessary.

Most of the activities have been successful with a broad range of students between the ages of eleven and eighteen, consequently it is quite deliberate that specific age groups have not been recommended.

It will be worth bearing in mind that whilst the order of exercises within each section is interchangeable, the more technically and physically demanding activities generally appear towards the end of the chapters.

The layout and design of the book is intended to give instant visual impact to help inspire the students, hence the emphasis on cartoons, but the notes are mainly aimed at the leaders and teachers. The book therefore has a dual purpose. Students should not normally be expected to work through these exercises alone. Some ideas for indoor activities have been included which are intended for the students to use.

The approach to outdoor work in this book has two main fundamentals which should be apparent in all of the pages. These are firstly to ensure that the students have <u>fun</u> in their work, and secondly that the exercises allow <u>all</u> individuals to be actively <u>involved</u> within their capabilities.

The following points give further information and guidance relevant to outdoor education generally:
1. <u>The Country Code</u>. As a point of some importance, 'The Country Code'

may be found on page 13. If activities and games are not always successful, all will not be lost if the students at least show that they understand and respect the rules of the Country Code.

2. Equipment. The safety of the students depends largely on the generous provision of appropriate protective clothing and equipment to suit the nature of the activities and the outdoor conditions. Detailed lists of equipment are not included, as this information is contained in many of the well known outdoor handbooks, manuals and reference books, such as those listed at the back of this book. Much valuable outdoor work can be done in the local environment however, without the need for expensive equipment and clothing.

3. Parents' Consent and Insurance. Schools, clubs and centres will all have their own particular procedures regarding outdoor work. In most cases it will be necessary to inform parents of the intended activities and to gain their consent. Insurance cover should also be arranged for the majority of work suggested in this book.

4. Group Size. All the exercises and games in the six chapters are designed for small groups. A MAXIMUM group size of ten students to one adult leader is strongly recommended. In wild country and in adverse weather conditions, the group size should be considerably smaller.

5. Leadership. With the exception of canoeing, most of the exercises and games contained in the first five chapters could be attempted by leaders and teachers who are fairly new to this sort of work, providing that their initial ventures are not too ambitious. Suggestions for teaching basic canoeing are found in Chapter Six.

It may help to try out the activities with a group of friends, or with one or two students when the opportunity arises. For those who intend to become quite involved in this work, there is no substitution for plenty of personal experience in the likely situations to be encountered. Further helpful notes about leadership are included in each of the six chapters, but those who are aiming to take their students out into wild and mountainous country should consider training for the 'Hill Walking Leader's Certificate', awarded by the Mountain Walking Leader Training Board.

6. Preparation. There are no short cuts in outdoor work with young people. Thorough preparation, even for local work, is essential for reasons of safety and for the general success of the venture. In general, most students would benefit from some involvement in the planning stage, the amount of which depends on the nature and level of difficulty of the exercise. To give some idea of the depth of preparation required for camping expeditions, leaders should refer to 'The Duke of Edinburgh's Award Scheme Expedition Guide'.

A considerable amount of preparation time is required even for <u>local</u> outdoor work. For example an orienteering training exercise in the school grounds, lasting one hour, would require a prepared base map of the area, a suitable training course, duplicated worksheets, and an explanation of procedures and rules.

7. <u>Reconnaissance Visit</u>. A piece of sound advice which has proved valuable on many occasions, is to visit the area in advance, in order to study the general layout of the area, the possibilities for training exercises, and the potential dangers and hazards.

8. <u>Alternative Plans</u>. It is advisable to have some alternative ideas in mind in case the original plans need to be altered. The usual reason for having to abandon activities is the weather. Many unexpected problems tend to spoil the original plans, and these could be disastrous for the venture unless alternative activities have been planned. To give a few examples, permission may unexpectedly be withdrawn for using a training area, the minibus may break down, or one member of the group may suddenly become ill.

9. <u>Discipline</u>. It is with some regret that I feel the need to add a word of caution. Despite the planning and organisation that goes into outdoor education and regardless of how much effort is made to make the exercises enjoyable, some students will still be inclined towards what they might think of as mischief, but what leaders might consider harmful or dangerous to themselves, to other members of the party or to the countryside generally. It is very important that leaders know their students, and occasionally exclusion might prove a safer option in preference to injury or desecration of the countryside.

10. <u>Accidents</u>. The Author and The Publisher can not be held responsible in any way for accidents or injuries which occur in the course of these games and exercises. The leader or teacher with responsibility for the group should ensure that the activities in this book are interpreted in a safe and reasonable way by <u>all</u> individuals involved. Leaders and teachers involved in any outdoor work with young people should be familiar with the booklet 'Safety in Outdoor Pursuits', produced by The Department of Education and Science.

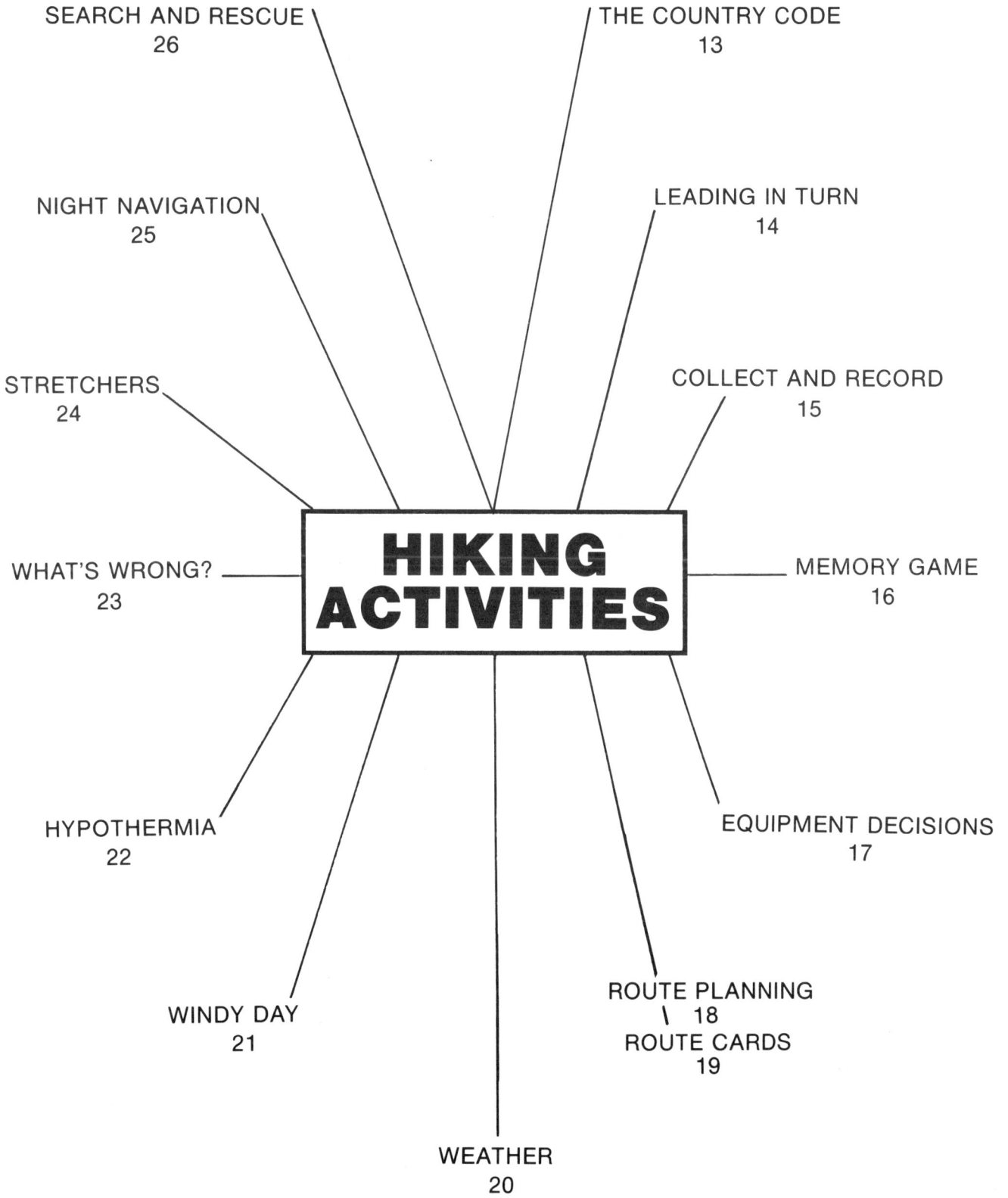

CHAPTER ONE

HIKING ACTIVITIES

All of the exercises in this chapter are intended to combine map navigation with some planned activity during the hike.

Even when working with complete beginners, all students in the group should be given some responsibility for navigating a small section of the hike, with the leader at hand to give advice and instruction. As map and compass skills are developed, the group may be given more demanding navigation routes to tackle, with or without the leader at hand, depending on the nature of terrain, weather conditions, group equipment, and the level of responsibility of the group.

The philosophy behind this chapter aims to offer a variety of interesting and useful tasks within a planned navigation walk. Most of the exercises included here have been chosen for their 'fun' value, but they would also help towards the development of more aware, prepared, and confident individuals.

This chapter offers a few ideas which may be used in a short local hike, which may well be in park land or in quite mild countryside near to the edge of town. The same ideas could also be used with groups working in mountainous regions.

Group leaders are recommended to refer to the more well known books for more detailed and technical advice, such as Eric Langmuir's Mountaincraft and Leadership, Alan Blackshaw's Mountaineering, and The Duke of Edinburgh's Award Scheme Expedition Guide. The Ordnance Survey 1:25,000 or 1:50,000 maps are also an obvious essential requirement to accompany this chapter.

The recommended ratio for groups involved in hiking activities, is a MINIMUM of 1 experienced leader to 10 students, and preferably more than one leader, especially when working in wild countryside. It will be apparent that most of the activities here will require a considerable amount of preparation time, plus continuous communication and encouragement throughout the sessions if they are to be successful.

THE COUNTRY CODE

The importance of the country code cannot be overemphasised. The leader has responsibility for teaching the rules of the country code at an early stage in outdoor work. Some of the rules may need to be stressed several times during the course of a day or at the start of each session. A natural way to start the group thinking about the country code is at a rest stop as shown in the sketch.

LEADING IN TURN

Although the idea for this exercise is borrowed from mountain leadership training procedures, this navigation and leadership experience can be equally valuable for younger groups.

Procedure: At the start of the walk, the adult leader would brief the group on leadership responsibilities. This would include - keeping the group together, following the rules of the country code, checking equipment and clothing, and accurate navigation. Depending on the aims of the venture, it is recommended that all individuals in the group are given adequate practice in map reading and setting a compass bearing from the map.

During the walk, the adult leader would give each individual, or pair, responsibility for navigating and leading the group for a given leg of the route. All members of the group should be encouraged to navigate throughout the walk, even though it may not be their turn to lead.

Venue: The idea can be used in all kinds of terrain, depending on the ability or experience of the group; i.e. parkland, woodland areas with many paths and tracks, moorland areas with few paths, etc.

Value: Leadership experience, map and compass navigation skills, communication, group responsibility, self confidence, decision making.

COLLECT AND RECORD

Procedure: ① Give each team a list of 15 items to find along the route, a map of the route, and a record card to complete along the way. Each team will also need a plastic bag or jar with ventilation holes in top, in which to keep the specimens.

② Make sure that all students can identify the 15 items, and stress the importance of collecting live (undamaged) specimens, see sample list below.

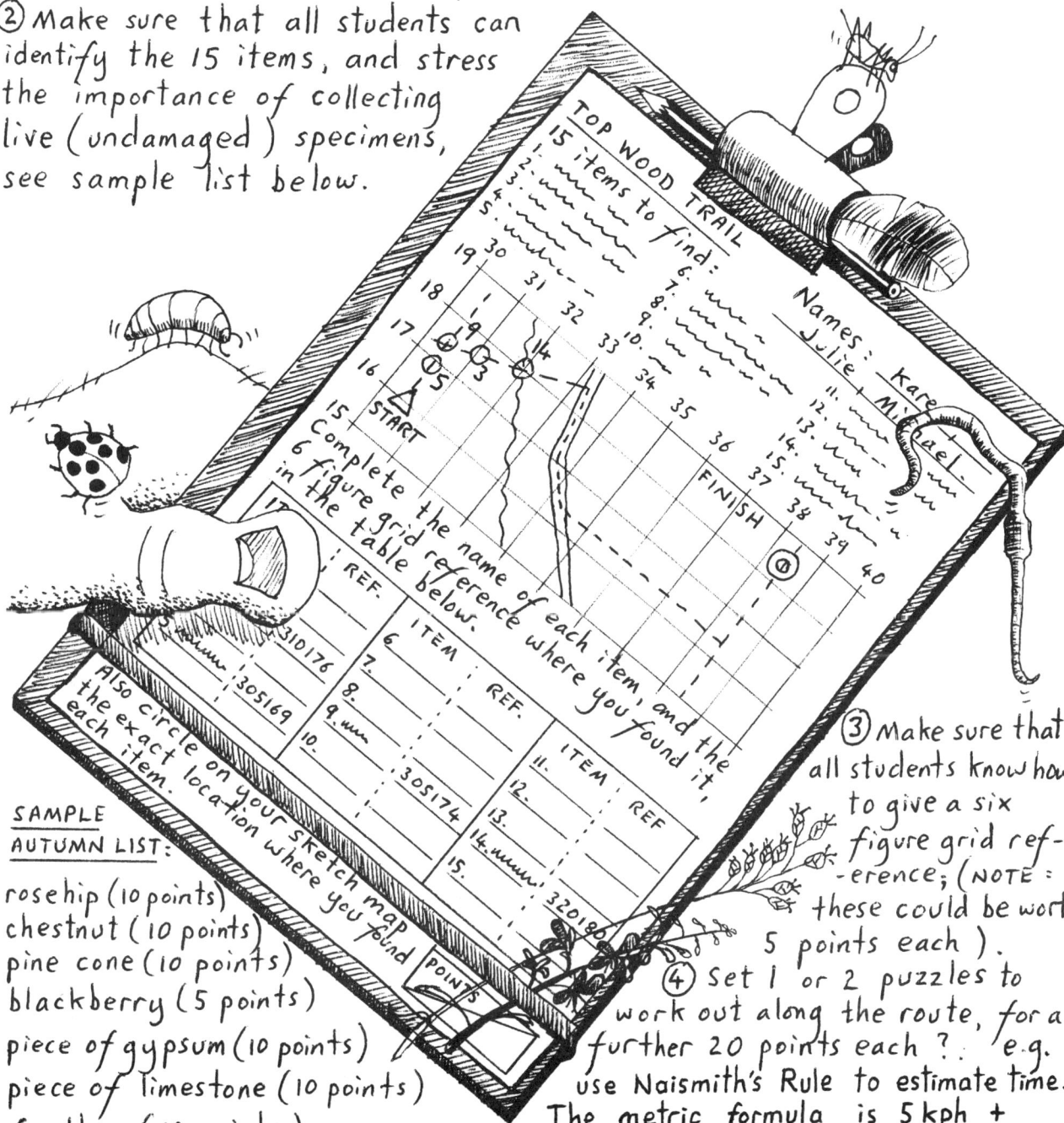

TOP WOOD TRAIL

15 items to find:
1.
2.
3.
4.
5.
6.
7.
8.
9.
10.
11.
12.
13.
14.
15.

Names: Karen
Julie + Michael

START
FINISH

Complete the name of each item, and the 6 figure grid reference where you found it, in the table below.

ITEM	REF.		ITEM	REF.		ITEM	REF
	310176	6.			11.		
	305169	7.			12.		
		8.			13.		
		9.			14.		
		10.		305174	15.		320180

Also circle on your sketch map the exact location where you found each item.

POINTS

③ Make sure that all students know how to give a six figure grid reference; (NOTE: these could be worth 5 points each).

④ Set 1 or 2 puzzles to work out along the route, for a further 20 points each? e.g. use Naismith's Rule to estimate time. The metric formula is 5 kph + ½ hr per 300 metres climb.

⑤ At the end of the walk, set aside some time for studying some of the samples, and then release the live specimens, being careful not to damage them. Some of the items could be carried back to base to make a display.
NOTE: Special care should be taken not to include rare flora and fauna in the list.

SAMPLE
AUTUMN LIST:

rose hip (10 points)
chestnut (10 points)
pine cone (10 points)
blackberry (5 points)
piece of gypsum (10 points)
piece of limestone (10 points)
feather (10 points)
snail shell (20 points)
blackberry/unripe (5 points)
rose-bay willow-herb (5 points)
evergreen leaf (5 points)
sycamore leaf (5 points)
live, undamaged worm (20 points)
live, undamaged insect (20 points)
live, undamaged wood louse (50 points)

MEMORY GAME

This is a useful exercise to throw in at a rest stop on the hike. The leader divides the group into two teams. The first team is instructed to lay down an anorak, and place 15 items on it. The items may be selected from pockets, rucksacks, and from the immediate area. The second team is then given 15 seconds to memorise the 15 items. After they have been covered up, the second team must attempt to write down as many of the items as possible in 2 minutes. After the list has been checked, the teams change over, and team 1 attempts to achieve a higher score (if possible).

MAP MEMORY - Another memory exercise can be done as the group walk along. The leader asks one member of the group to look at the map, and memorise 5 features which the group will pass, along his or her leg of the route. These features must then be identified (without further reference to the map. The next member of the group then chooses another 5 features, and so on.

EQUIPMENT DECISIONS

This training exercise may be completed indoors or in the area close to the base. The aim of the exercise is to provide opportunities for decision making and handling equipment. The exercise may take 30 minutes to prepare, and about one hour to complete, but it should be worth the effort. A maximum of 10 people is recommended, + 2 leaders.

Procedure :

① Before the group arrive, lay out all the equipment and waterproofs needed for a summer hill walk. Bags or containers with labels may be used as substitute items if necessary.

② Divide the group into teams of 4 or 5. Two people from each team collect all the items for their team.

③ The leader then announces that the group are about to start their imaginary walk. The weather is dry and sunny and they must pack their rucksacks, but first they must decide as a team, exactly where each item will be placed.

④ When both teams are ready, the whole group may start to walk around a set route. At a suitable point, the leader would stop the group and instruct them to put on their waterproofs, as a heavy rainstorm has suddenly started. Those people who had already put on their waterproofs or who had packed them at the bottom of their rucksacks, would be given 10 penalty points. Others receive 10 bonus points.

⑤ The group then continues along the walk. At the next point, the leader stops the group and asks them to set a compass bearing from their map. Those who had their map and compass inside the rucksack would be given 10 penalty points. Those who were ready would receive 10 bonus points.

⑥ The group then continues along the walk. At the next point, the teams could go through the routine of making an imaginary brew of tea, using small stove and other items from inside the rucksacks, then rucksacks would again be packed. At this point, the leader having observed both teams, could give out more penalty points and bonus points, for tidyness and rucksack packing.

⑦ The group continues along the walk again. At another suitable point, the leader would inform the group that one person from each team has suddenly become seriously ill, and two people from each team must prepare to walk 10 miles across the hills to telephone for a doctor. Each team must decide exactly which items will stay with the casualty and friend, and which items will be packed when two people go off for help. After the rucksacks have been packed, the leader may discuss this final problem, and give out more penalty points and bonus points. ⑧ Finally, all items would be checked back in, important points re-capped, and team totals worked out.

ROUTE PLANNING

Route planning should be an important part of any training programme for hiking activities. The hypothetical exercise on the next page, attempts to simplify the awesome task of completing a full, detailed route card.

The format given may be used as a basic outline for use with a variety of maps and routes. The group leader will need to fill in alternative answers, as shown in the example route card. The students are then required to cross out the wrong answers, by studying each leg of the route, shown on an overlay.

EQUIPMENT : Ordnance Survey maps, set of route cards (with 2 alternative answers completed each time), overlays - with points circled and numbered, and route marked, compasses, pencils, paper or string to measure distance.

VALUE = specific map and compass skills - including : reading 6 figure grid references, identifying map symbols, measuring distance, using a scale, estimating heights, estimating time, setting grid bearings and converting to magnetic bearings, identifying suitable escape routes.

ROUTE PLANNING - CONTINUED

(hypothetical exercise)

Note: The standard format for the route card is shown in CAPITAL - LETTERS. Alternative answers have been written in small letters and underlined. Grid References have been left blank.

ROUTE CARD No. 3 (Cross out the wrong answers)
POINT ① (GRID REFERENCE 123456) TO POINT ② (_____).
POINT ① AT THE START OF THE ROUTE, IS A car park? / camp site?
THE DISTANCE BETWEEN POINTS ① AND ② IS ½ km? / 1 km?

POINT ② (GRID REFERENCE_____) TO POINT ③ (_____).
POINT ② IS AT A path junction? / bridge?
THE DISTANCE BETWEEN POINTS ② AND ③ IS 1 km? / 1½ km?
THE ROUTE BETWEEN POINTS ② AND ③ follows a stream? / climbs a slope?

POINT ③ (GRID REFERENCE_____) TO POINT ④ (_____).
POINT ③ IS AT a stream junction? / hill summit?
THE DISTANCE BETWEEN POINTS ③ AND ④ IS 2 km? / 1 km?
THE MAGNETIC BEARING BETWEEN POINTS ③ AND ④ IS 90°? / 180°?
THE ROUTE BETWEEN POINTS ③ AND ④ follows a ridge? / crosses a road?

POINT ④ (GRID REFERENCE_____) TO POINT ⑤ (_____).
POINT ④ IS AT A small lake? / small wood?
THE DISTANCE BETWEEN POINTS ④ AND ⑤ IS 2½ km? / 1½ km?
THE MAGNETIC BEARING BETWEEN POINTS ④ AND ⑤ IS 270°? / 200°?
THE ROUTE BETWEEN POINTS ④ AND ⑤ follows a rocky edge? / goes downhill?
THE HEIGHT AT POINT ④ IS 300 metres? / 200 metres?

POINT ⑤ (GRID REFERENCE_____) TO POINT ⑥ (_____).
POINT ⑤ IS AT A stream junction? / road junction?
THE DISTANCE BETWEEN POINTS ⑤ AND ⑥ IS 1 km? / 1½ km?
THE MAGNETIC BEARING BETWEEN POINTS ⑤ AND ⑥ IS 15°? / 50°?
THE ROUTE BETWEEN POINTS ⑤ AND ⑥ crosses a brook? / climbs a slope?
THE HEIGHT AT POINT ⑤ IS 50 metres? / 100 metres?

THE TOTAL DISTANCE OF THE ROUTE IS 8 km? / 6½ km?
THE TIME TAKEN TO COMPLETE THE WALK (AT A PACE OF 4 km PER HOUR)
IS 4 hours? / 2 hours? [NOTE: TIME SHOULD BE ADDED TO THIS FOR
CLIMBING HILLS AND RESTS.] A SAFE ESCAPE ROUTE FROM: point ④,
would be to follow the stream - path in a northerly direction to
the road? / point ④, would be to climb down the steep slope
to the south?

WEATHER

All outdoor groups should be encouraged to develop an interest in weather forecasting, as their activities may need to be modified in relation to the daily forecast. This practical session at the base is intended to give students first hand experience of collecting various kinds of weather information.

Listen to a pre-recorded tape, (or video?), of the general forecast for the following day; e.g. Radio 4, 5-55 p.m., and make notes under specific headings.

Make specific notes from the daily weather map, and find out the meaning of the figures and symbols on a station circle.

Phone the weather station for your region, and make specific notes.

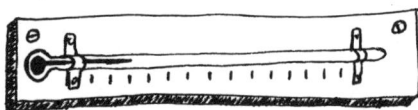

Record the outdoor shade temperature in degrees celcius, using a dry bulb thermometer.

Record the cloudiness outside in oktas - e.g. 2 oktas or ¼ cloud cover.

Identify the type of clouds visible.

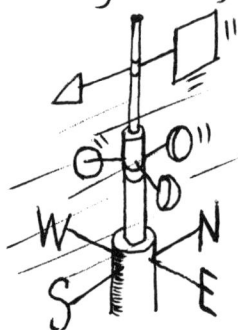

Record wind direction using an improvised wind vane, (made by the students?).

Record wind speed using an improvised anemometer and Beaufort Scale.

Depressions - Find out the sort of weather associated with depressions.

Air Pressure - If a barometer is available, record air pressure and note any change in pressure?

Further work - Find out how temperature, wind, cloud and rain change in hilly areas.

At the end of the session ask for volunteers to use their recordings to plan and present a T.V. style weather forecast for the day.

WINDY DAY

A windy day can present good opportunities for testing qualities of resourcefulness, perseverance and cooperation. The aim of this exercise is to design and construct a wind shield, (indoors?), and then to test the effectiveness of the wind shield by boiling a kettle of water out in the open.

Procedure :   ① At the base, the group may be divided into two teams, and they are given the materials, (strong polythene, string, tape, scissors, bamboo canes, etc), to design and construct a type of wind shield which will offer protection on three sides.
The stove with kettle in position, may be set up so that dimensions can be estimated. Tape and string may be used to attach the polythene to the canes. The final product should be collapsable, so that it can be carried in or on a rucksack to the test site.
② All the necessary items for making a mug of tea should be packed, and a suitable navigation walk planned.
③ While some members of the group are setting up the wind shields and lighting the stoves, another team could use a large sheet of polythene and cord to improvise another LARGE wind shield to shelter the group. NOTE: Special care should be taken in strong winds, to avoid FIRE spreading to the wind shield and vegetation.

HYPOTHERMIA

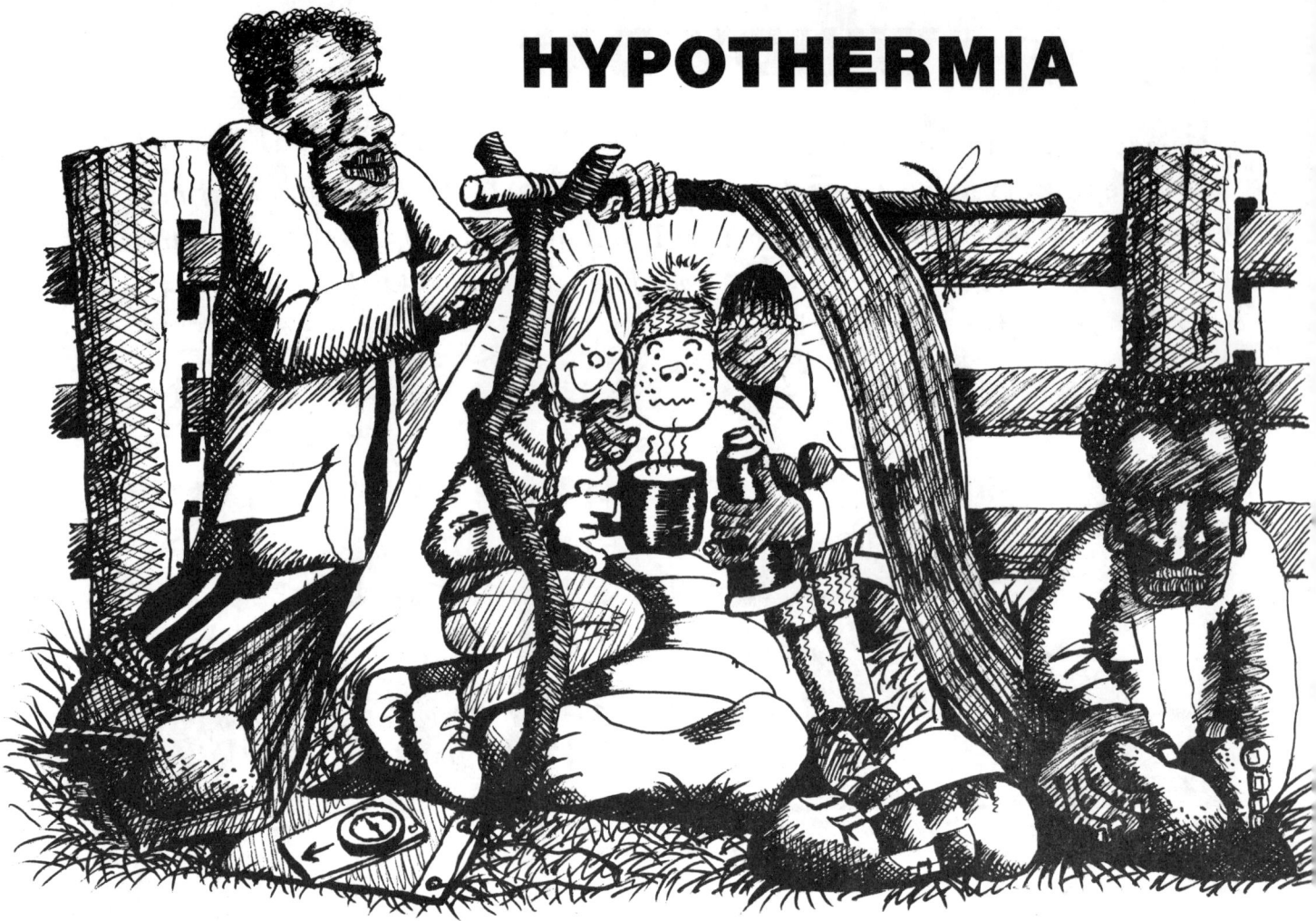

Procedure: A little instant acting is required for the success of this multi-problem exercise. At the start of the walk, the leader could brief the group on the causes of hypothermia, and the signs, symptoms and treatment. This information is best shown on a laminated card, (refer to first aid books or mountaineering books). The group could then be informed that at some stage during the hike, one member of the group would start to show the obvious signs of suffering from hypothermia. The leader would discretely choose one individual to act as the hypothermia casualty. The other members of the group would be expected to respond in a responsible manner and work quickly as a team to make the casualty warm, and to improvise a shelter. The group would also be required to complete an accident message card which would involve the use of an Ordnance Survey map to note the exact location, and to work out a suitable route for some members of the group to send for a doctor.

Equipment needed for each group: Laminated information and instruction card, lengths of cord, large polythene sheet for improvised shelter, survival bag, hot drink in flask or stove and kettle, etc, Ordnance Survey map, map case, compass, pencil, accident message card with spaces to fill in, additional clothing and equipment depending on weather conditions and terrain.

Value: Initiative, caring for others, problem solving, instant acting, communication, outdoor survival, safety awareness, teamwork, map reading, thoroughness.

WHAT'S WRONG?

(A day in the hills!)

What should be the correct way?

STRETCHERS

At a pre-planned point during the walk, a card may be given to the group, with instructions, explaining how to cope with a suspected fractured leg. This group initiative exercise would also involve the construction of an improvised stretcher, preferably using items that have been carried, or dropped off in advance.

The group would also be required to write out an accident message card, which would involve the use of an Ordnance Survey map to note the exact location, and to plan a suitable escape route.

After the padded splint has been strapped to the patient (see first aid books for correct method!), and the stretcher has been checked by the leader, the group may then plan a simple obstacle course to test the ability of the group to carry the stretcher and patient safely. One penalty point could be given for each fault on the obstacle course. The obstacle course should not be too hazardous, or the stretcher patient may need real treatment! The stretcher should only be carried at walking pace, taking care to keep the patient horizontal at all times.

Equipment needed for each group:

Laminated instruction card, 2 × 6 foot poles and 2 × 4 foot poles, lengths of lashing cord, strong plastic sheet or survival bag for stretcher mattress, Ordnance Survey map, compass, map case, accident message card with spaces to fill in, pencil, splints, improvised padding and wrapping.

Value: Teamwork, initiative, caring for others, problem solving, fun, communication, outdoor survival, safety awareness, perseverance.

Note:

This exercise is especially suitable as an assessment task, using some of the above criteria.

24

NIGHT NAVIGATION

Courses planned on public paths and bridleways in fairly mild countryside, can present an attractive challenge at night. The following procedure list was given to all members of my group at an essential training meeting before a night navigation exercise.

<u>Note</u>: It may be necessary to inform the local police and farmers or land owners of your plans.

<u>Procedure</u> : ① Before you start, check that you have all the necessary items - including map, control card, compass, watch, whistle, torch, spare batteries and anorak. ② Before you start, write your names on the control card, and fill in your time out, final return time, and emergency phone no.
③ You will be timed out in pairs. You must keep together throughout the course. Your control card will NOT be signed at the check point cars unless you are together. ④ You must keep to the route shown on the map. The route is on public paths and minor roads. Do not attempt to cut across any farmland or woods, as these are PRIVATE !
⑤ Be sensible - i.e. keep as quiet as possible - especially near farms and houses, close all gates, do not drop any litter and do not flash your torch around too much. Remember, we will need to use this area again in the future ! ⑥ The main aim is to complete the course by checking in at each of the three check point cars in order.
⑦ Do not be too hasty. Be absolutely certain of your position on the map at all times. Double check your intended direction of travel at each point. Hold your map so that it is pointing in the direction you want to travel.
⑧ Do not follow other pairs without checking your own map. They may be lost ! ⑨ If you are completely lost, weigh up the situation calmly, and if you still feel unsure about moving on, retrace your steps to a known point. Do not split up. ⑩ If you have wandered completely out of the area, you are completely lost and you are over the final return time, find a telephone and phone the emergency number shown on your control card, (or the police). Do not split up. ⑪ If you become ill or have an accident, make your way to the nearest check point car if you are capable. If you cannot do this, keep as warm as possible and call for help + flash torches until help arrives. Do not split up.
⑫ You must report to the finish and hand in your control card, map, compass, etc, even if you do not complete the course.

ENJOY YOURSELF, BUT BEWARE OF THE MONSTER !

SEARCH AND RESCUE

This multi-problem exercise always seems to be appealing to young people. The exercise tends to be most exciting at night, in unfamiliar country, although successful search and rescue exercises can easily be planned in daytime in a park or on paths near the edge of a town.

Procedure: A card is given to the group with a message - i.e. ' injured and exhausted person located at grid ref. 211359 (wall corner); make padded splint for sprained or fractured ankle, keep patient warm and comfortable, and help back to base by most suitable route'. The group should be given full responsibility for organising the search party with necessary clothing and equipment, navigating accurately, caring for the patient (which may involve constructing an improvised stretcher, and returning to base as a group. Two or three groups could be involved in similar exercises at the same time, each group navigating to different points. Value: group responsibility, teamwork, caring for others, initiative, resourcefulness, communication, navigation, perseverance. Note: On one memorable night exercise in Derbyshire, when I was acting as the injured person out on the hillside (making realistic moaning and groaning noises), the group had become so involved in the exercise, that one girl broke down in tears when their torches finally shone upon my prostrate form.

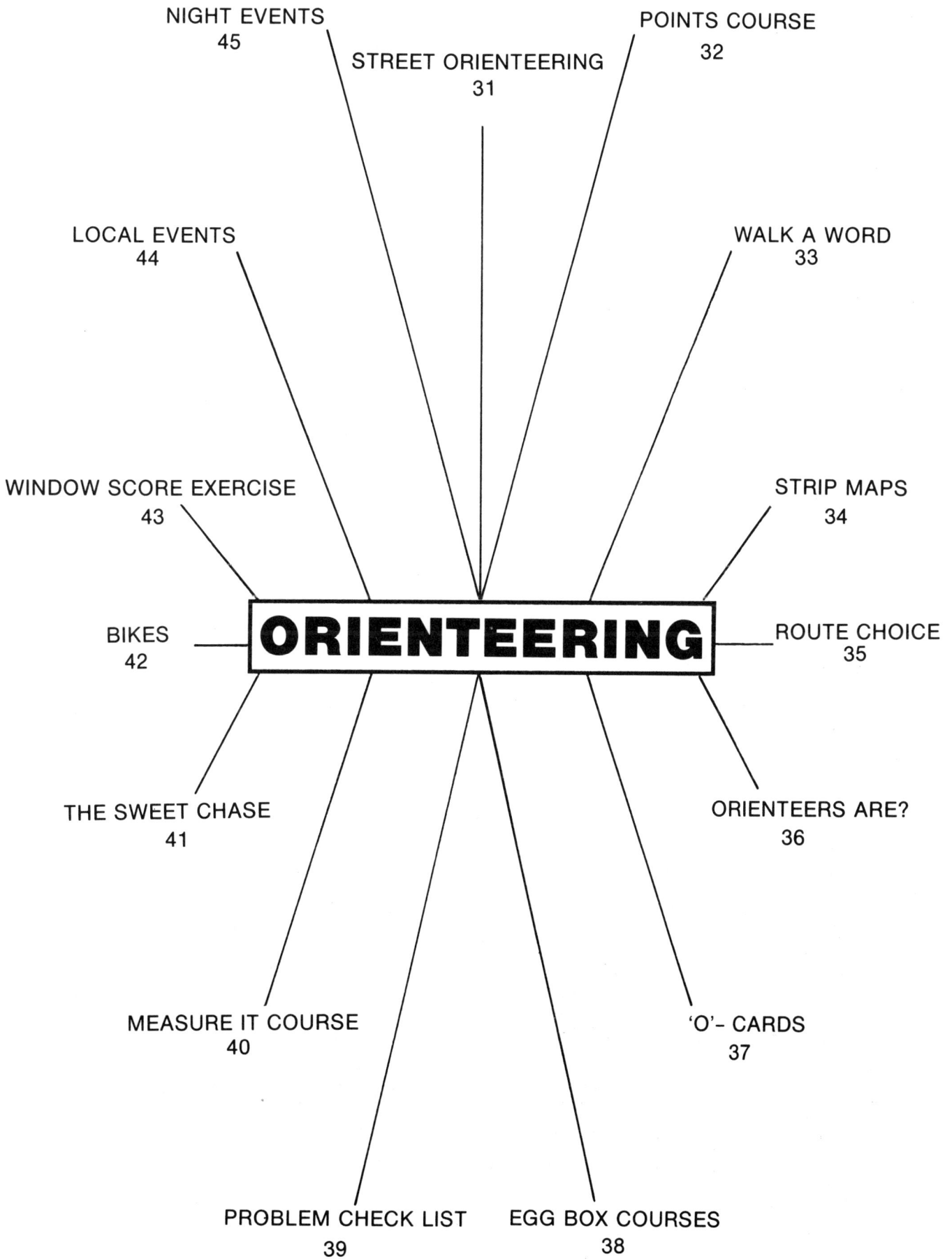

CHAPTER TWO

ORIENTEERING

In this chapter I have attempted to provide a sample of training exercises and ideas for beginners' groups. The exercises have been designed, especially for groups with limited opportunity for travelling to interesting orienteering areas. Many of the ideas may bear little resemblance to true orienteering, as they are a compromise, to fit a number of particular situations.

If the group is restricted to an urban base, then several indoor and outdoor exercises are still possible. Indoor sessions could make use of orienteering maps with courses marked on them. These are especially valuable for route choice practice, and symbol recognition. There are also many possibilities for indoor orienteering games. Pages in this chapter include: 'egg-box courses', 'route choice', and 'o-cards'.

Map reading in the urban area near the base can also be very successful with groups. 'Street orienteering'- as explained in this chapter, may give some ideas for working out courses.

If the group can travel to a nearby park, or open area with public paths and bridleways, then the possibilities become more interesting. Exercises designed for areas such as these, include - 'strip maps', 'measure it course', 'points course', and 'window score exercise'.

The group may be fortunate enough in having a leader who will take them to an event, organised by their local orienteering club?

For group leaders who are thinking about orienteering as a possible new activity, may I suggest two initial steps :
i) try out a few events yourself, join your local orienteering club, and make contacts with other club members who may offer help or advice;
ii) read some of the more well-known orienteering books, such as - 'Orienteering' by John Disley, 'Your Way with Map and Compass - Orienteering' by John Disley, 'Know the Game Orienteering'- produced in collaboration with the Scottish Orienteering Association, 'Mapmaking for Orienteers' by Robin Harvey, and 'Teaching Orienteering', A Handbook for Teachers, Instructors and Coaches, by Carol Mc Neill, Jean Ramsden and Tom Renfrew.

IMPORTANT POINTS

1. A Balanced Programme. The exercises and ideas contained in this chapter are intended to be used along with other more familiar orienteering training exercises, to make up a balanced, comprehensive beginners' course.
The leader will need to plan his or her programme, depending on the needs of the particular group, and the resources available.

2. Preparation. As with other activities in this book, orienteering with groups requires a large time commitment for the leader. Thorough planning and preparation are essential for successful orienteering at any level.

3. Access. Most of the training exercises outlined here, may be done near the base, or on local public paths or parks, where permission may not be required. If group leaders are planning more ambitious events, in private woodlands or other orienteering areas, then written permission from the landowners is ESSENTIAL. Your local orienteering club will be able to give advice on suitable areas to use. Any thoughtless action, involving trespass, could result in the loss of valuable areas for thousands of orienteers!

4. Supervision. The very nature of orienteering requires the individual to navigate alone, with map and compass, through the countryside. This statement may be true for experienced orienteers, but for many young beginners' groups, I would suggest a more controlled approach at first.

Initially, the leader could walk around a simple course with the group, showing them how to read and hold the map, and how to conduct themselves out of doors. This controlled stage is valuable for keeping an eye on progress and behaviour.

The leader's method could be changed in the next session, by accompanying the group around the first half of the course, and then timing them out in pairs for the second half of the course.

If satisfactory progress is made after a few training sessions, then suitable courses could be attempted, with the students navigating in pairs, or alone. Even when the students are given maximum freedom for orienteering, the leader should always be fairly close at hand, to give help and supervision, when necessary.

5. Group Size. Where possible, groups should be small, with a suggested maximum of 10 students to one leader.

6. Code of Conduct. The importance of the country code should be stressed with all groups. This is particularly necessary for young orienteers who will be given the responsibility for finding their way around the countryside, without close supervision.

7. Success. An important point worth remembering when introducing students to orienteering is the fact that they need not be athletes to be successful. Unlike crosscountry running, the orienteer is alone in the forest competing against himself or herself. For many orienteers the feeling of achievement in navigating successfully around a course is sufficient reward for their efforts.

Don't be put off! Orienteering can be great fun.

BEGINNERS' TRAINING MAPS

The two maps on this page are intended to show how simple it is to produce basic training maps suitable for young beginners. These black and white maps show only the essential information needed for youngsters to find their way on paths and tracks around a suitable safe area with public access. Students may progress onto courses using the detailed colour orienteering maps by arrangement with local orienteering clubs. Note especially that contour lines have been completely omitted from these beginners' maps, and alternative symbols and labels used to show hills and slopes.

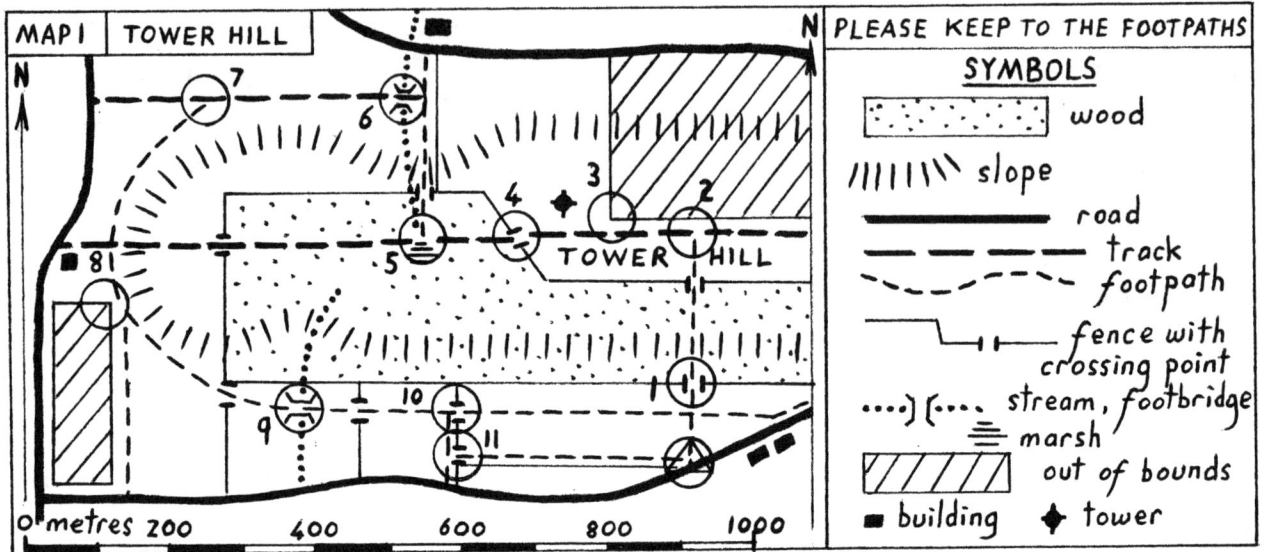

A similar map to the one above can be produced by first making a simplified tracing from a 1:10,000 Ordnance Survey map, and then checking and modifying details in the field. The completed tracing is then photocopied, and the course pre marked on the maps in red biro. The students will also need a control description list with spaces for the codes to be written in at each control marker.

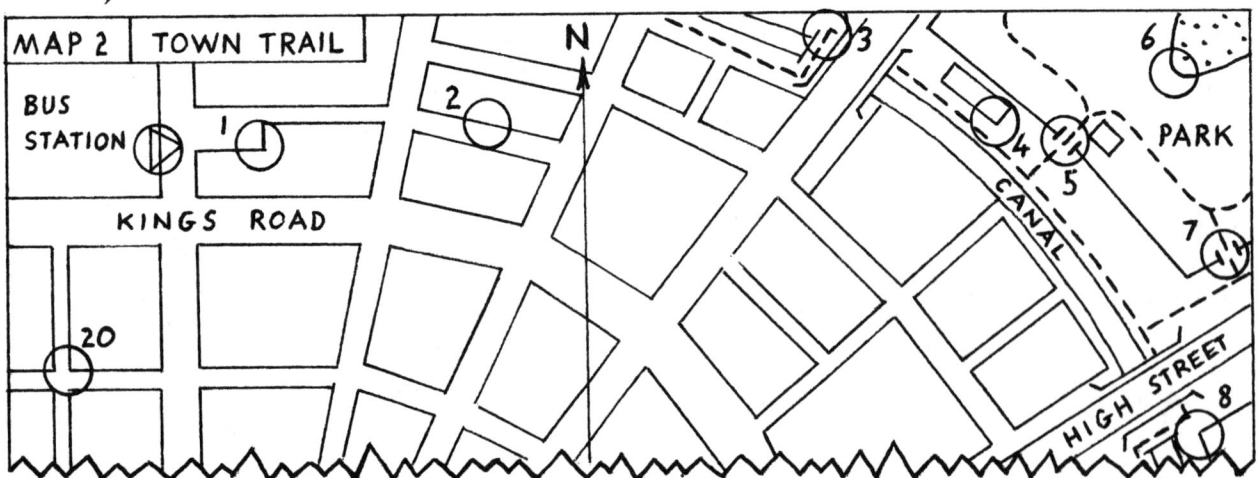

Map 2 shows part of a simple street orienteering map. Notice how most of the street names have been removed to encourage map reading techniques.

IMPORTANT : Map makers must follow the copyright guidelines when Ordnance Survey and other maps are used. For more detailed advice on mapmaking, refer to Robin Harvey's book, 'Mapmaking for Orienteers' obtainable from the British Orienteering Federation.

STREET ORIENTEERING

POINT ① The steps.
How many steps?

(198, 199)

Here are some examples of the sort of question that could be asked on a street orienteering course.
Each question could be given a points value, and the aim is to gain as many points as possible.

POINT ② Church spire
What feature is at the top of the spire?

GRRR!

POINT ③ Hall entrance
What stone animal is found at this point?

POINT ④ Hotel hanging sign
How many people are painted on the hanging sign?

POINT ⑤ Market square (centre)
Sketch the design set into the pavement.

TRAVELLER'S REST

POINT ⑥ Archway
What building can you see through the archway?

BILL'S BAKERY
FAST DELIVERY SERVICE.

POINT ⑦
Corner building
In what year was this building built?

1844

Many towns and villages produce large scale street maps (often at little or no cost), showing tourist information, bus routes, or conservation areas, etc. These may be ideal for street orienteering, although they will need to be pre-marked and sealed in plastic bags, so they may be used again.

POINTS COURSE

An important feature of any course designed for beginners, should be that it allows everyone to experience the feeling of achievement. An obvious way of providing for this, is to see that the control flags or markers are located mainly on the paths and tracks (line features), and not hidden away in the middle of the forest.

Another way of designing an orienteering course for beginners, is to give each control a set number of points, depending on the degree of difficulty, or the distance away from the start. The beginners then aim to gain as many points as possible, within a time limit, and all is not lost if some of the controls have not been found.

Pairs or individuals are timed out at intervals, and timed in, but their overall time is not as important as points on this particular type of course.

The job of checking progress along the course is much easier if the course is planned so that competitors visit the controls in a given order, as shown below, in the completed example.

NORTH COMMON POINTS COURSE		NAME(S): Jenny Green and Linda Smith		
TIME OUT : 11-00 a.m.	FINAL RETURN TIME : 1-00 p.m. (YOU MUST RETURN BY THIS TIME !)			
CONTROL ORDER	DESCRIPTION	CODE LETTER	POINTS	
1	path junction	Y ✓	5	
2	path / track junction	A ✓	10	
3	stile (crossing point!)	Z ✓	15	
4	footbridge	H ✓	15	

NOTE 1 : The students will need a training map (similar to map 1 on page 30) with the course premarked in red biro. NOTE 2 : This is basically a normal cross country orienteering course with an additional points bonus for each control.

WALK A WORD

The idea of this game is to set out the capital letters of an unknown word, on the ground, by following instructions - giving directions (or compass bearings), and paces. A long piece of string is layed out in the shape of each letter, (or chalk may be used on hard surfaces.)

Note: Always start facing north. All letters start on an imaginary base line. Some lines return along the same path, to make the string continuous for each letter, (e.g. letter E = Ǝ). Some method of keeping the string in position may be needed, e.g. pegs or sticks.

Each pair could be given a card with instructions for only one word, to reduce the chance of forward planning. Each new word becomes progressively more difficult, i.e. using different letters, longer words, longer paces, and compass bearings.

Example ①

LETTER ①
N.W. × 6 paces,
S.E. × 6 paces,
N.E. × 6 paces.

LETTER ②
N.E. × 6 paces,
S.E. × 3 paces,
W. × 3 paces,
S.E. × 3 paces.

LETTER ③
N. × 5 paces,
S.E. × 7 paces,
N. × 5 paces.

(Compass rose: N, NE, E, SE, S, SW, W, NW)

Example ②
(with compass bearings)

LETTER ①
30° × 5 paces,
150° × 5 paces,
30° × 5 paces,
150° × 5 paces.

LETTER ②
90° × 4 paces,
270° × 4 paces,
0° × 2½ paces,
90° × 4 paces,
270° × 4 paces,
0° × 2½ paces,
90° × 4 paces.

LETTER ③
45° × 6 paces,
125° × 3 paces,
270° × 3 paces,
90° × 3 paces,
125° × 3 paces.

LETTER ④
0° × 5 paces,
270° × 2 paces,
90° × 4 paces.

STRIP MAPS

STAGE ①

Each pair is given a small section or strip of map to complete as they walk along a path or track.

Accuracy is not essential for this exercise. The idea is to observe the features on either side of the path or track, and mark these onto the strip map. A simplified list of black and white orienteering symbols will be needed.

Note: The leader will need to prepare several different outline strip maps with only paths and tracks marked on.

STAGE ②

Each pair should also set out 3 or 4 red and white orienteering markers, on suitable features next to the path. These points should be circled and numbered on the strip map. The markers should be clearly visible from the path.

Note: It may be necessary for the students to make up some symbols if they find any useful features which are not shown on their symbol sheet.

STAGE ③

Back at the start, maps are checked, and then exchanged with another pair. Each pair should now have a new strip map with symbols drawn on, and a simple 3 or 4 point orienteering course marked onto the map. The markers are to be found and collected, using the map drawn by another pair.

Note: A simple pacing exercise would be useful in preparation for this activity. As the strip maps will be surveyed at walking pace, the students could count how many double walking paces it takes them to cover a measured distance of one hundred metres.

ROUTE CHOICE

This game is intended for two players.
Each player, in turn, carefully marks a route
around the course, on a copy of the page.
Each player moves one square at a time, and
records the points for each square in the grid
at the bottom of the page. The aim is to achieve
the lowest total score for the full course.
The numbers in the squares, represent the
degree of difficulty of the terrain. Two routes
may go through the same square, and routes
may cross over, but they must not go through
the intersection points of the squares.

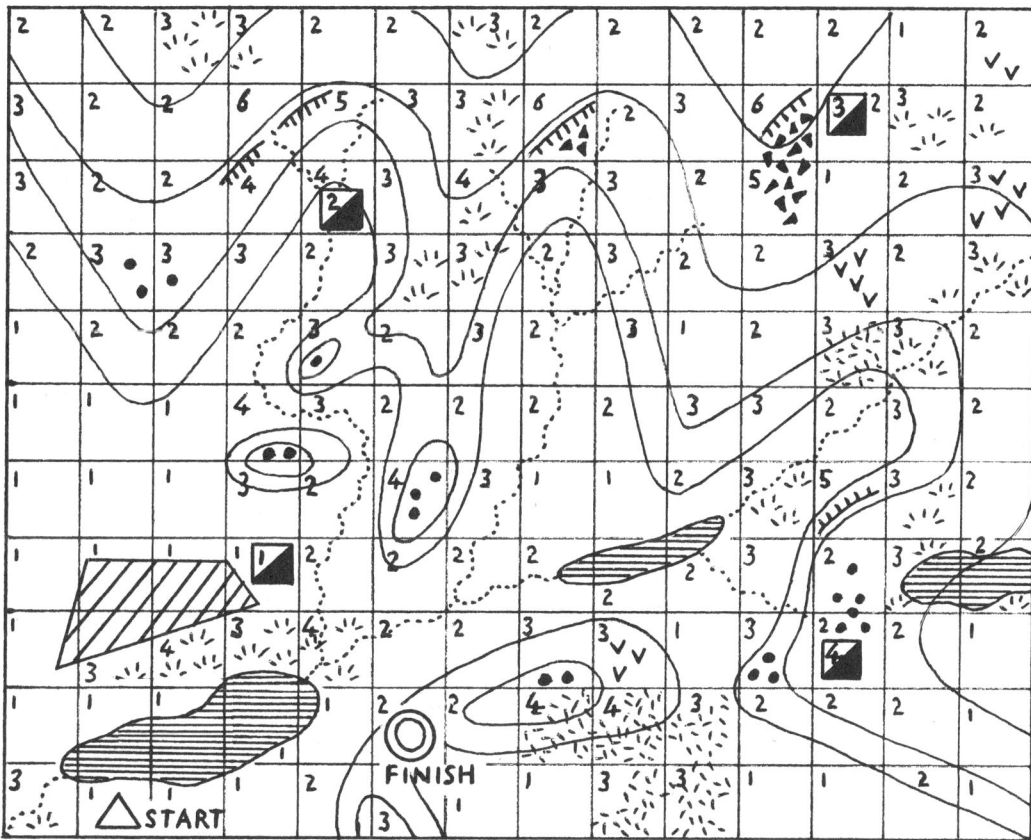

START

FINISH

SYMBOLS : ▨ fenced enclosure (out of bounds), ⸜⸝ crossable marsh
⸱⸱⸱ crossable stream, ⬭ lake (not crossable), ⌇ contours, v pit,
⌓ steep slope, ◣ boulder field, ⸛ dense thicket, • knoll.

PLAYER ①													TOTALS
LEG 1													
LEG 2													
LEG 3													
LEG 4													
LEG 5													
									GRAND TOTAL				

PLAYER ②													TOTALS
LEG 1													
LEG 2													
LEG 3													
LEG 4													
LEG 5													
									GRAND TOTAL				

Finally, compare your routes, with those of other people in the group.
This page may be re-produced, so that several pairs can play the game.

ORIENTEERS ARE?

Which words do you think apply to topclass orienteers?
Complete a questionnaire to see what other people think in your group.

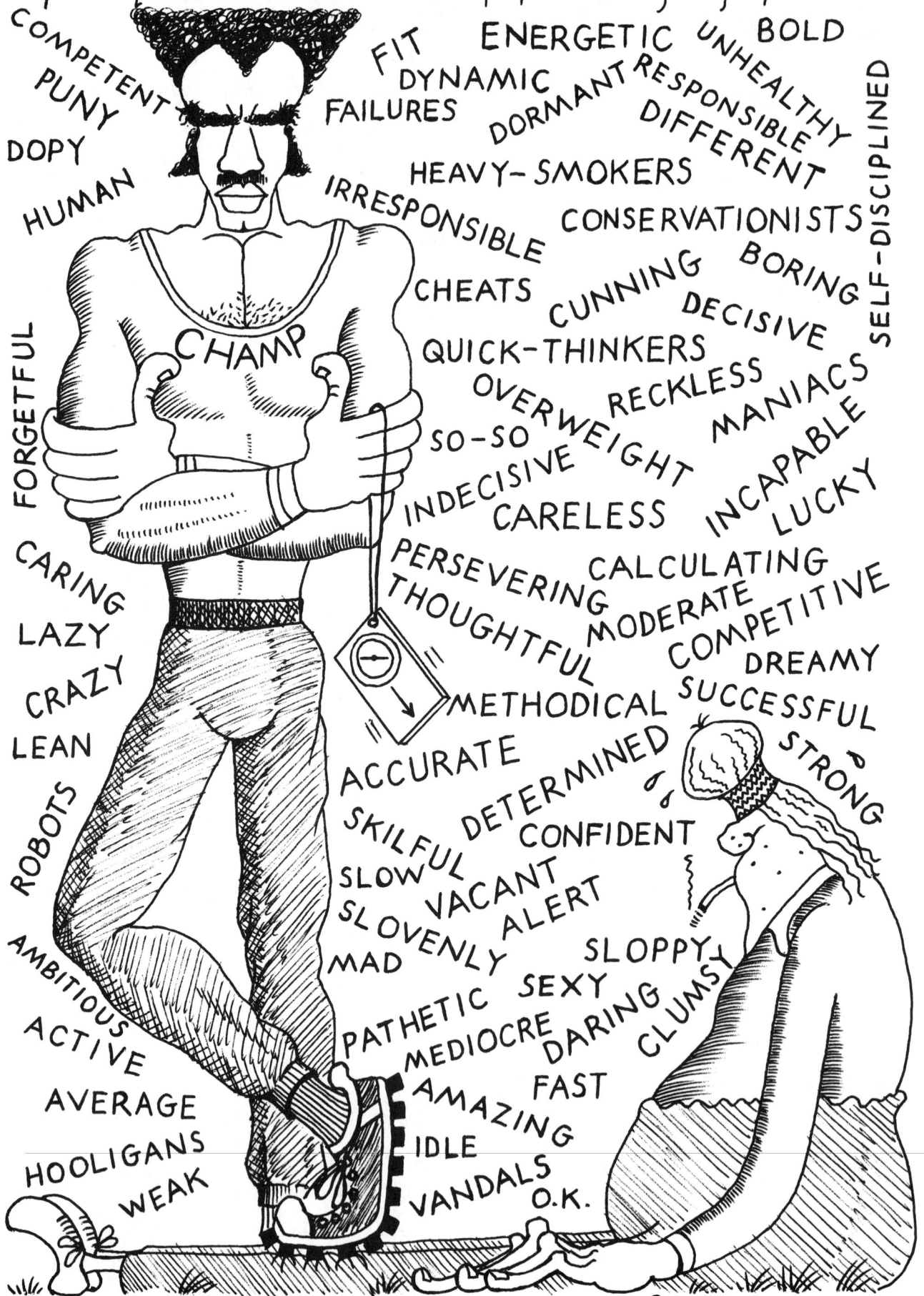

COMPETENT
PUNY
DOPY
HUMAN
FORGETFUL
CARING
LAZY
CRAZY
LEAN
ROBOTS
AMBITIOUS
ACTIVE
AVERAGE
HOOLIGANS
WEAK

CHAMP

FIT ENERGETIC BOLD
DYNAMIC UNHEALTHY
FAILURES DORMANT RESPONSIBLE
HEAVY-SMOKERS DIFFERENT
IRRESPONSIBLE CONSERVATIONISTS
CHEATS CUNNING BORING
QUICK-THINKERS DECISIVE
OVERWEIGHT RECKLESS MANIACS
SO-SO INDECISIVE INCAPABLE LUCKY
CARELESS
PERSEVERING CALCULATING
THOUGHTFUL MODERATE COMPETITIVE
METHODICAL SUCCESSFUL DREAMY
ACCURATE DETERMINED STRONG
SKILFUL CONFIDENT
SLOW VACANT
SLOVENLY ALERT
MAD SLOPPY
PATHETIC SEXY DARING CLUMSY
MEDIOCRE
FAST
AMAZING
IDLE
VANDALS O.K.

SELF-DISCIPLINED

Which words would you like to describe yourself?

'O'– CARDS

This card game is intended to remind the players of some of the more important orienteering skills, and common errors made, during a competition. First of all, a set of 30 normal size playing cards needs to be made. One side of each card is shaded red and white, to represent a typical orienteering control flag, and the other side is printed, as shown below.

THE 16 PENALTY CARDS (minutes are added on for these cards).

RUSHED! PENALTY +10 minutes	POOR MAP READING. PENALTY +5 minutes	POOR CONCENTRATION. PENALTY +5 minutes	FOLLOWED SOMEONE TO WRONG CONTROL. PENALTY +5 minutes	TIRED ON CLIMBS. PENALTY +10 minutes	FOLLOWED SIMILAR PATH (PARALLEL ERROR). PENALTY +10 min.	DIDN'T READ CONTOURS. PENALTY +10 minutes	DIDN'T TAKE COMPASS BEARING. PENALTY +15 min.
INJURY. PENALTY +20 minutes	DIDN'T READ CONTROL DESCRIP-TION. PENALTY +5 min.	TOO CAREFUL. PENALTY +5 minutes	TURNED COMPASS 180° OUT. PENALTY +15 minutes	MAP DAMAGED. PENALTY +10 minutes	SYMBOL MISREAD. PENALTY +5 minutes	WANDERED AROUND SEARCHING AIMLESSLY (LOST!) PENALTY +30 min.	NO DETERM-INATION. PENALTY +20 minutes

THE 8 BONUS CARDS (minutes are subtracted for these cards).

GOOD ROUTE CHOICE. BONUS −20 minutes	ACCURATE COMPASS BEARING. BONUS −15 minutes	'AIMED-OFF' PURPOSELY TO ONE SIDE. BONUS −10 min.	OBVIOUS FEATURE (ATTACK-POINT) USED. BONUS −10 min.	ACCURATE PACE COUNTING. BONUS −15 minutes	'HANDRAIL' FEATURE USED, e.g. wall, path or stream. BONUS −10 min.	CONSTANT SPEED MAIN-TAINED. BONUS −30 min.	NO TIME LOST AT CONTROLS BONUS −10 minutes

(ALSO, 6 BLANK CARDS ARE NEEDED)

The cards are shuffled, and layed out at random, on a table. The cards are scattered around a **START** triangle card. The red and white sides face upwards. This arrangement could represent a 'score' course, with the control flags set out around the start. Each player, in turn, picks up any card, reads out the comment, and then places the card on his or her pile. If a **PENALTY** card of say 15 minutes is picked up, then a marker is moved along the score card (see below) to add on 15 minutes. Both players start at 100 minutes. If a **BONUS** card of say 10 minutes is picked up, then a marker is moved backwards, to subtract 10 minutes; this player then has an extra go, after a bonus card has been picked up. The **WINNER** will have the shortest time, after all cards have been picked up.

THE SCORE CARD (Each player needs a small marker to move backwards or forwards)

5	10	15	⁓	90	95	START	105	JIM	⁓	275	280	ROB	290	295	300

EGG BOX COURSES

This practical exercise requires students first to create their own relief map, using egg boxes, and then to plan their own orienteering course and route. Each pair will need a large sheet of paper or card for the base, egg boxes or egg tray, scissors, pens (blue, black, red), and paper for writing out the control descriptions.

Procedure :
① Examples of simple relief features and landforms are shown, using the cutup egg boxes , (e.g. - valley, pass, ridge, spur, corrie, knoll, peak, etc.).
② Cut up the egg boxes and lay out the shapes onto the base. Draw around the shapes, when you are satisfied with their positions.
③ With a blue pen, mark 3 rivers (+ 4 bridges ⌒)(⌒), 3 lakes ⬭, and 3 marshes ⸴⸴ ⸴⸴. ④ Plan an orienteering course with 10 to 15 control points, + start and finish, and mark these in red biro; (see - examples of orienteering courses before you start. There should be some route choice problems for each leg of the course).
⑤ With your red biro, make a dashed line to show the best route around the course. With your black biro make a dashed line to show an alternative route.
⑥ Make a list of control descriptions for your course, e.g. 1 = spur, 2 = lake, N. side ; 3 = pass, etc. (Refer to list of terms and sample descriptions.) ⑦ Finally, volunteers' talk their way around their course, (to the rest of the group), giving a description of the route, and reasons for the routes chosen.

Further Activity: Draw contour lines around each of the shapes.

PROBLEM CHECK LIST

	course 1.	course 2.	course 3.	course 4.
Name of area				
Date				
Course distance in km				
Time				
Position				

Look again at each leg of your orienteering course, on your map.
Shade one small box to show each time you had a problem.

		course 1.	course 2.	course 3.	course 4.
① Did you have any problems reading the map?					
② Did you use the map all of the time ?					
③ Did you set (orient) your map at each control point ?					
④ Did you make any mistakes with your compass ?					
⑤ Did you choose a bad route at any time ?					
⑥ Did you feel very tired at any time ?					
		course 1.	course 2.	course 3.	course 4.

Look again at your completed check list. What do you think are the three most important ways to improve ?
Note: This page may be reproduced to use as a record sheet.

MEASURE IT COURSE

Each pair will need a piece of string 1 metre long, which is marked every 10 c m. Instead of looking for the normal red and white orienteering flags, a measurement is made with the string, at the points marked on the map. This style of course has the obvious advantage that flags or markers need not be set out beforehand. The students will need a training map (similar to map 1 on page 30) with the course premarked.

WEST PARK MEASURE IT COURSE	NAMES :

① Gate post. Measure the distance around the large left hand gate post. _____ c m.

② Brick building. Measure the full height of the brick building. _____ metres, and _____ c m.

③ Footbridge. Measure the exact length of the footbridge. _____ metres, and _____ c m.

THE SWEET CHASE

The layout of this event is the same as a normal orienteering 'score' course, but the competitors have an additional bonus at each control site, - a SWEET!

The red and white control flags or markers are set out around the start/-finish area. The controls which are further away from the start are given a higher points value than the controls nearer the start. Competitors have complete freedom to work out their own route around the controls, They should visit as many control sites as possible, in order to accumulate maximum points in the time allowed.

To make the event even more competitive and exciting, a sweet is hung at each control site. A few larger 'goodies' could be hung at random control sites.

The controls should be set out in such a way, that from the 'MASS START', there are numerous approaches that can be taken, and the competitors hopefully will split up, and aim for different control sites.

Those who reach a control first, will find a sweet hanging off the flag or marker, but they will need to show the 'wrapper, as evidence at the finish, in order to gain a bonus 50 points. Unlucky competitors who reach a control site after the sweet has been removed, will still gain some points, by writing down the code letter, or punching their control card.

BIKES

Real cycle orienteering presents many organisational problems, e.g., is there a suitable area nearby?, will the land owners give us permission?, how do we get the bikes to the event?, do we have enough bikes?, how large an area do we need?, what sort of map will be needed?

The following exercise attempts to overcome some of the practical problems, by scaling down the nature of the event.

VILLAGE CYCLE TRAIL

LOGISTICS : ① A local village, with quiet roads and back streets, can make an ideal venue, without the need to seek permission from land owners. ② Simple observation questions could be set at say 10 or 15 points. This method avoids the need to set out control flags. ③ A large scale, clearly drawn street map will be needed, with the control points circled and numbered. ④ The cyclists may visit the controls in a given order, or, a free choice of route may be preferred, depending on the particular circumstances.

SAFETY : ① Most groups will need official approval or authorisation, before cycling can proceed. ② As this exercise is intended to take place on village roads and streets, there will always be unexpected dangers from other vehicles. Rules and safety precautions must be strictly observed. ③ Racing is NOT necessary. Emphasis should be on safe, careful cycling, alone, or in pairs. ④ Groups should be small. There should be no more than seven cyclists to one leader. ⑤ All cycles should be checked by the leader, to see if they are in a roadworthy condition. **NOTE :** BMX bikes are NOT suitable for this activity.

WINDOW SCORE EXERCISE

This is an interesting way of using a small, well known area, for basic orienteering practice. As shown in the example below, only a small part of the map is shown in the 'window' around each control. Sufficient detail is given inside the windows to allow students to navigate between controls. The exercise is mainly intended to practice direct navigation, using compass bearings and pacing, so it would be necessary to check that there are no major obstacles in between the windows.

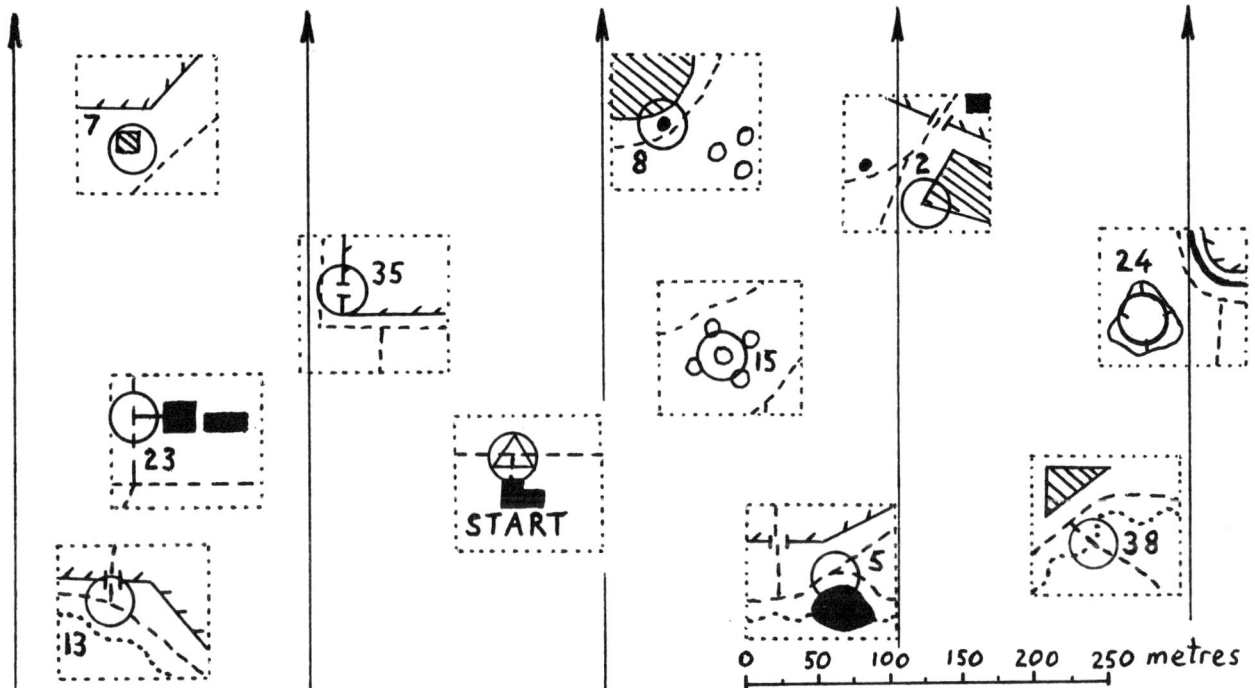

(Part of a map to show a possible design for a window score exercise)

This is also designed as a 'score' exercise, which means that competitors should aim to score as many points as possible, in a given time limit, by visiting the controls in any order.

The controls which are further away from the start, should be given a higher points value than the controls nearer the start. There is no set course or order of controls, so competitors are faced with the additional problem of choosing their own route. The whole group may be started at the same time.

Simple cardboard markers could be made by the group, for this training exercise. Their initials could be used as code letters.

<u>Note</u>: Competitors will also need a control description list, with points, and spaces to write down the code letters. This exercise is based on Tony Thornley's 'Window Orienteering' Training Event as shown in O-Tech Sheet No.1, published by the British Orienteering Federation.

LOCAL EVENTS

Most of the training exercises in this chapter are intended to lead up to local events organised by orienteering clubs in your region. Local events normally offer a variety of courses, ranging in difficulty from the easy short courses for beginners, to the more demanding longer courses for experienced orienteers. These courses are normally colour coded according to their level of difficulty, with the white and yellow courses being the easiest. People can usually turn up on the day and enter for these events.

PERMANENT ORIENTEERING COURSES. These are rapidly gaining in popularity throughout the regions. They provide a valuable training resource for orienteers of all ages and standards. Further details about Permanent Orienteering Courses can be obtained from 'Compass Sport Magazine', Permanent Course information, 37 Sandycoombe Road, Twickenham, Middlesex TWI 2LR.

To find out more about orienteering and events in your area, send for the general information pack from: British Orienteering Federation, "Riversdale", Dale Road North, Darley Dale, Matlock, Derbyshire DE4 2HX.

NIGHT EVENTS

Many orienteering clubs organise night events or training exercises in the winter evenings. This type of orienteering is great fun, and very challenging. It is advisable to check with the organiser, before the event, to see if they can cope with the numbers in your group. It is also advisable to invite only the students who have had some previous orienteering experience, as these night events are normally much more demanding.

CHAPTER THREE

MONSTER STORY
63

SHOP AND AUCTION
50

MENU PLANNING
49

BIVOUACS
62

SPAMBURGERS
51

FLY-SHEET
61

TENT PITCHING
52

CAMP ACTIVITIES

SARDINES
60

POCKET JACKET
53

CAMP FIRE MUSIC
59

RAW EGGS
54

THE SENTRY GAME
58

WHAT'S WRONG?
55

PRISONER
57

EXPEDITION CAMP?
56

CAMP ACTIVITIES

This chapter offers a few ideas which may be fun to do on camp, after the day's activity has been completed.

Some pages are intended as preparation exercises for the camp; these include – 'menu planning', 'what's wrong?', and 'expedition camp?' Some of the activities in this chapter could be included in a camp crafts course, and are therefore suitable for groups working at, or near to the base, in the weeks leading up to a planned camp.

Teamwork and co-operation are always important on camp, and so several team – problem solving tasks have been included which are intended to test these qualities; these tasks include – 'tent pitching', 'fly sheet', and 'pocket jacket'.

Pages such as 'monster story', 'camp fire music' and 'bivouacs', are open to the leader's own interpretation, and so no explanation has been given. Indeed, all of the ideas in this book may need to be modified or improved, to make them suitable for any particular group or situation.

Many important aspects of camping have been missed out of this chapter, as they lie outside the scope of this book. Group leaders involved in camp activities will obviously need to spend time working with their students on such essential routines as – lighting instructions for stoves, safety procedures around the camp site, care of equipment, the country code, and other rules.

MENU PLANNING

Plan your menu for a 3 day camp,

and estimate the costs.

SHOP AND AUCTION

Both of these exercises are intended to give the group first-hand experience of handling a variety of equipment and clothing, usually found in a camping shop.

CAMPING SHOP

Two students take on the role of shop assistants, and another student is required to be a customer - who will come into the shop and ask for advice on one or two pieces of equipment. The shop assistants must then be as convincing as possible, giving the customer all the usual sales talk. The customer could be the awkward type - who needs to know all about the equipment before he will decide.

CAMPING AUCTION

Volunteers take turns at acting as auctioneer. A starting bid is agreed upon, and the rest of the group must raise a hand to increase the bid. The auctioneer should aim to point out some of the qualities of the equipment, and try to keep up the fast speaking style.

SPAMBURGERS

TENT PITCHING

Tent pitching can be made into a group problem solving activity. The exercise can be good fun, and the problem will make the group think!

NOTE :
A more formal approach is recommended for expedition preparation where safety of the group may depend on correct instruction.

Procedure :
1. Give each group a tent (that is strange to them), and give instructions to pitch the tent correctly, working as a team.
2. State that grades A - E will be given for teamwork, thoroughness in pitching the tent, and effort in packing away.
3. A word about the cost of the tent may be necessary to avoid any damage.
4. When all tents have been pitched, the whole group, with the leader, can inspect each tent in turn, giving criticisms and credit where appropriate.

POCKET JACKET

This is an amusing problem solving exercise which will take about one hour. The idea is to design and make a waistcoat with pockets to carry as many items as possible - i.e. tins, potatoes, apples, etc. Teams of 3 or 4 people could work secretly in separate places, and finally 'model' the finished garment in front of the others and the judges.

EQUIPMENT NEEDED
FOR EACH TEAM :
strong polythene sheet
scissors
marker pen
improvised needle
string
items - e.g. tins, potatoes, apples.

ASSESSMENT : Give grades A-E for - teamwork, design, practical skills, and holding capacity of pockets.

RAW EGGS

And now for something completely different ! ....
..........Try the raw egg eating competition ! ?

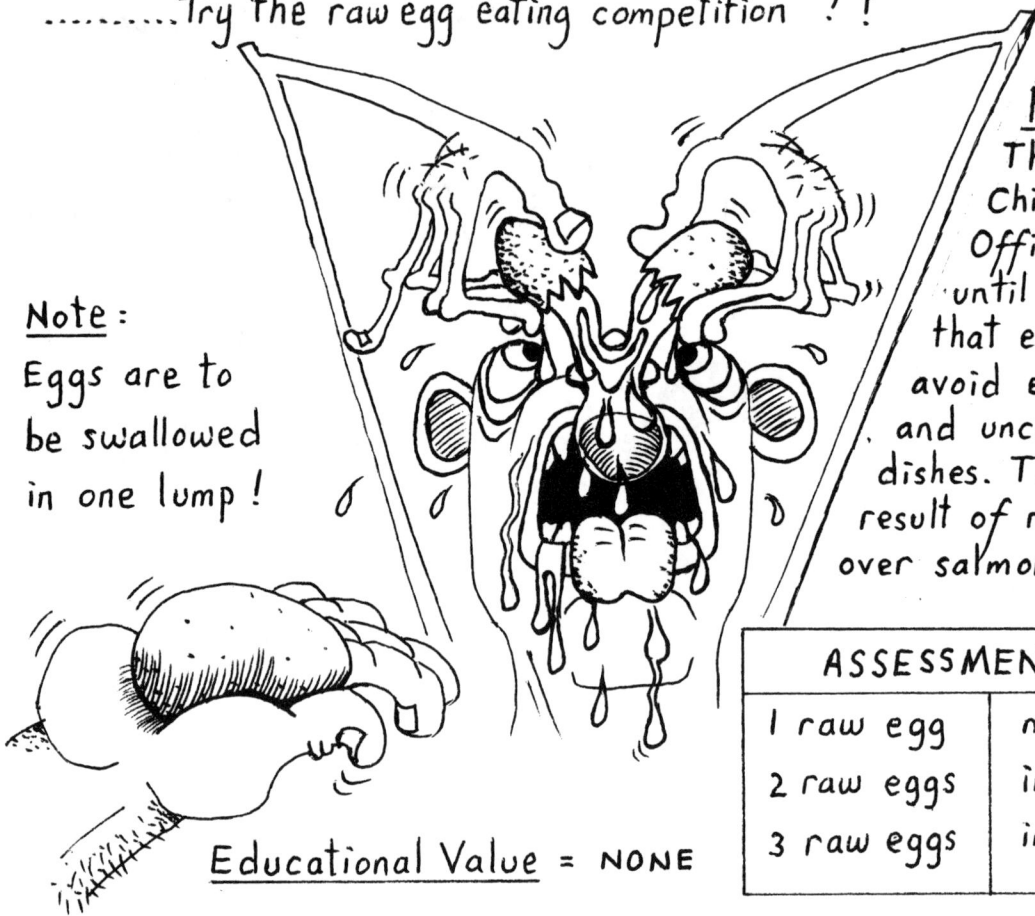

Note :

Eggs are to
be swallowed
in one lump !

Educational Value = NONE

Author's Footnote :

The Government's Chief Medical Officer has advised until further notice that everyone should avoid eating raw eggs and uncooked egg dishes. This is as a result of recent concern over salmonella poisoning.

ASSESSMENT SCALE	
1 raw egg	marvellous
2 raw eggs	incredible
3 raw eggs	impossible

STRETCH

The aim of this competition is to see who can place a tin the furthest distance away from a line, by the method shown in the sketch. The competitor must return to standing position without using knees or hand for support.

54

WHAT'S WRONG?

(inside the tent)

What should be the correct way?

EXPEDITION CAMP?

This group have just arrived at their expedition site after a long day on the hills. The site they have chosen is in a remote valley at about 500 metres above sea level. It is late autumn, and weather conditions are becoming worse – with strong cold winds, and heavy rain clouds approaching.

What are they doing wrong?
What should be the correct way?
What is wrong with their equipment?
What equipment should they use for high level expeditions?
What problems are they likely to face tonight?

PRISONER

The escaped prisoners will need plenty of places to hide within a radius of about 20 metres. Suitable locations could include woodlands, open bracken areas with large boulders, or open common land with many small land forms – such as hollows, mounds and small valleys, etc.

RULES OF THE GAME :   ① The group is divided into 'prisoners' and 'guards'.
② Everyone starts at the central point or prison. This could be a definite feature, such as a ruined building, or a circle made from stones.
③ The guards cover their eyes for 30 seconds to allow the prisoners to escape and hide.   ④ After 30 seconds, the leader signals for the guards to come out of the prison, and search for the escaped prisoners.
The guards may search for periods of say 30 seconds. When a prisoner is caught, he should be led back to the prison, where he must stay, unless another prisoner reaches in to touch him. ⑤ The guards will need to decide how many to send out searching. ⑥ The game continues until all prisoners are caught, then the teams change over.

THE SENTRY GAME

The sentry game is always a popular evening exercise on camp. There can be many variations to this game, depending on the features available in the area. The basic rules are as follows :- two teams are decided : one team is on sentry duty, and the other team is on a spying mission. The spies are given a white wool arm band at the start of the game. The spy team has to move along a set linear route, i.e. a wall, ditch, hedge, etc, without being caught by the sentry team. The sentry team can only look for the spies at a given interval, i.e. 30 seconds. The sentry team then has another time limit, of say 30 seconds, to locate as many spies as possible, and remove their wool arm bands to prove that they have been caught.

This game can bring out a number of dubious qualities in the youngsters (and the leaders!), but it can mainly be taken as a light-hearted exercise, requiring team co-operation, self control, concentration and cunning. One of my most successful attempts at this game, was on a particularly dark November night in the Derbyshire hills. The linear route chosen was a dry stone wall, and the only way through for the sentry team was via a sheep hole - only one metre high. Our group of rogues became so involved that the game continued well into the night, and the leaders' spy team (who had sportingly agreed to take part) ended up with more than their arm bands removed !

CAMP FIRE MUSIC

SARDINES

This is guaranteed to provide lasting memories. An element of surprise is required for the success of the operation.

When the group are inside their tents, and preparing for a normal night under canvas, the leader announces a change of plan! Everyone should bring their sleeping bags and torches, etc, for a night exercise. The group is then led to an interesting location for a "sleep-out", under the sky. Everyone sleeps side by side (like-sardines in a tin). Boys are directed to one site, and girls are directed to a separate site near-by.

Remember to check the weather forecast before the sleepout, and remember to bring a hat - to keep the insects off. Do not sleep inside a plastic survival bag!

FLY-SHEET

This is a useful exercise to test group co-operation and communication. The activity is also great fun to watch.

<u>PROCEDURE</u> : 1. Each team of 4 people is given a fly-sheet, poles and pegs, (or tent, poles and pegs).

2. Instructions are given for 2 people in the team to be blindfolded, and the other 2 people are to communicate how to erect the fly-sheet, without actually helping.

3. The leader awards grades A-E for co-operation, communication and thoroughness.

4. A further grade may be awarded for packing-up.

BIVOUACS

MONSTER STORY

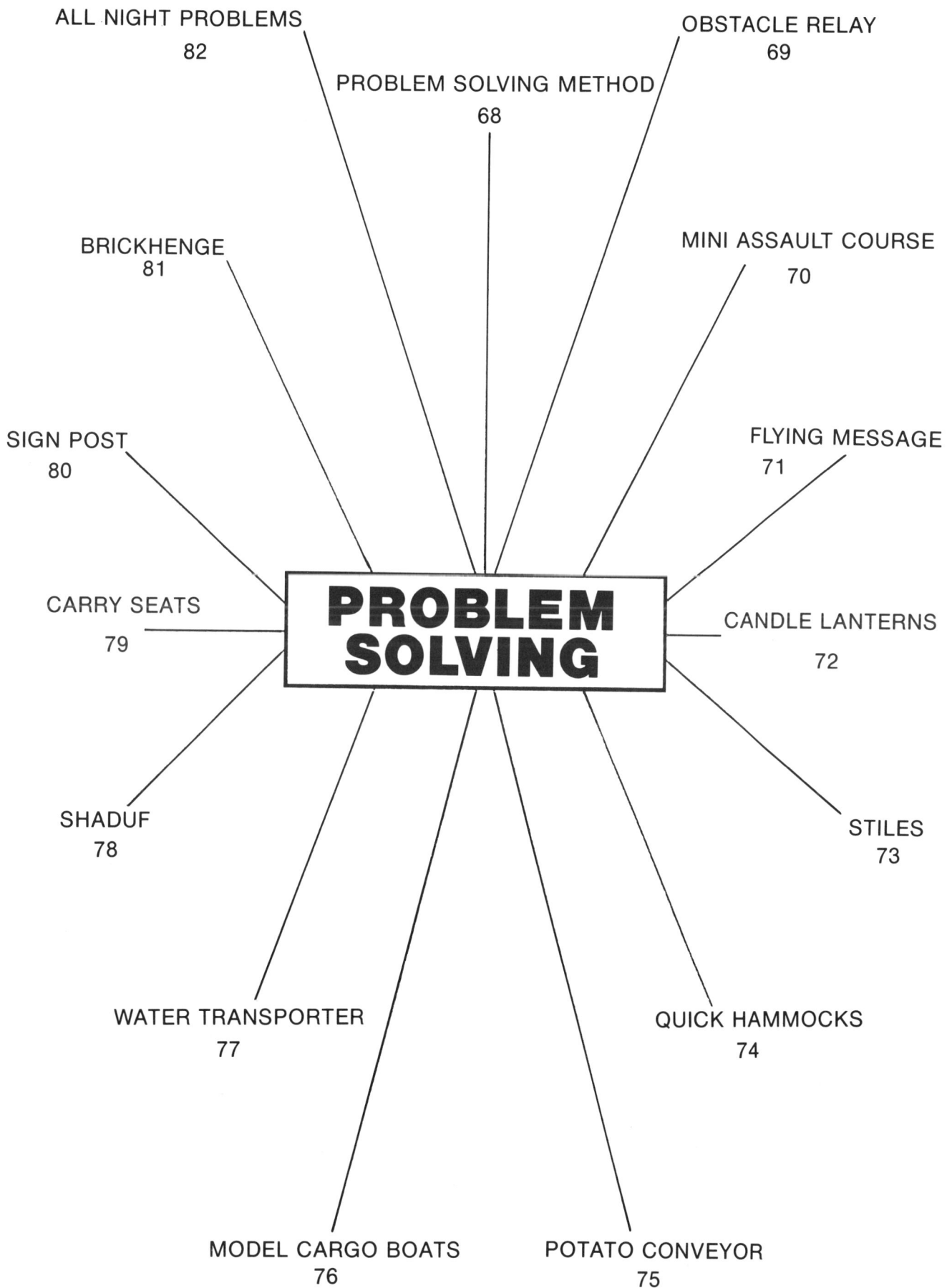

CHAPTER FOUR

ALL NIGHT PROBLEMS
82

PROBLEM SOLVING METHOD
68

OBSTACLE RELAY
69

BRICKHENGE
81

MINI ASSAULT COURSE
70

SIGN POST
80

FLYING MESSAGE
71

CARRY SEATS
79

PROBLEM SOLVING

CANDLE LANTERNS
72

SHADUF
78

STILES
73

WATER TRANSPORTER
77

QUICK HAMMOCKS
74

MODEL CARGO BOATS
76

POTATO CONVEYOR
75

PROBLEM SOLVING

Problem solving provides opportunities for students to cope with unusual situations. To be successful problem solvers, they must show some initiative, and be resourceful. The exercises in this chapter have been selected because of their appeal to young people.

A method of approaching problem solving is shown on the next page. I have found the two most important aspects to be, 'working as a team', and 'persevering'.

Problem solving may be done in many situations. It may be planned as an activity in a residential course, or camp. It may be used on a training course at the base, or as an evening fun session when the day's activities have been completed.

Each individual leader will have his or her own particular way of introducing an exercise to a group. A suggested way is to give the group a brief look at the sketch, to help motivate the students. The leader would then need to describe the problem, and hand out the equipment. The teams may then continue without further reference to the sketch, although the leader will need to be at hand to give encouragement. The easiest option in problem solving situations is to give up! For more experienced groups, it may be sufficient to briefly describe the problem, without any reference to the sketch.

Most of the basic equipment required for these exercises is easily obtainable from hardware or D.I.Y. stores. The wooden poles could be purchased through your Area Forestry Commission office, or from a garden centre. The poles do not need to be too thick and heavy for the exercises in this chapter; a maximum diameter of 7cm should be sufficient. Hard woods will obviously last longer than soft woods. The poles will also be useful for other exercises in this book, e.g. 'bivouacs' and 'stretchers'.

None of the exercises here will require any great strain on the ropes or lines. A recommended thin strong rope for lashing light poles together, and for other purposes, including the overhead rope in the 'water - transporter' exercise, and the main support ropes in the 'quick hammocks' exercise is an 8mm diameter, 3 strand hawser laid terylene rope. Lashing ropes for use with the light poles, may be cut up into ready lengths of 5 or 6 metres, with their ends sealed to prevent fraying.

The exercises are likely to be more successful if some time is spent practising knots. Useful knots to learn include: square lashing, diagonal lashing, reef knot, bowline, overhand loop, figure of eight loop, and round turn and two half hitches.

The Scouts have been problem solving (or 'pioneering') for many years. John Sweet's Scout Pioneering book, obtainable from Camping and Outdoor shops, contains a wealth of useful information on knots, equipment, and exercises (fully illustrated). This book is highly recommended for leaders who intend to develop their problem solving or pioneering.

The activities outlined here are not intended to show the only way of solving problems. Leaders and students are encouraged to adapt, and improve on these basic ideas.

All of the exercises in this chapter (with the exception of 'ALL NIGHT PROBLEMS') are straightforward enough to be attempted with minimum planning and organisation. 'ALL NIGHT PROBLEMS' has been intentionally left for the last page to indicate its level of difficulty. This final problem could well take several weeks of planning, training and organisation, before it is ready to be attempted.

Some leaders may prefer to assess their students on their problem solving skills, and others may do it just for fun. There is room for both approaches. Some of the stages illustrated on the next page could be drawn up into a grid, and used as an assessment record sheet, so that leaders and students may follow their progress over a period of time.

Finally, don't forget the camera! The students will enjoy looking at their problem solving capers captured on film.

PROBLEM SOLVING METHOD

Here are some stages which are intended to be used with each of the problem solving exercises in this chapter.

PLANNING AND DESIGNING

CONSIDERING ALTERNATIVES

WORKING AS A TEAM

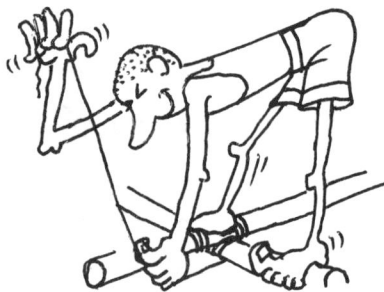

USING SKILLS AND KNOWLEDGE

PERSEVERING

I give up!

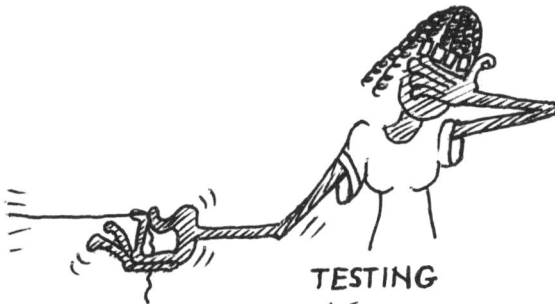

TESTING

MODIFYING

TIDYING

REFLECTING

ASSESSMENT: Some of these stages may be used as a basis for assessing the students. A grade A, B, C, D or E could be given for each stage to be assessed.

OBSTACLE RELAY

THE PROBLEM: To design and construct an obstacle course.
Each team should include 15 problems in their obstacle course. All courses should be about the same length. Each problem should be designed so that a blindfolded competitor can successfully move along the course, with a member of his or her team giving instructions from behind a line. Possible problems could include – stepping over, squeezing through, crawling under, changing direction, stepping between, picking up items, and carrying items, etc.

When the obstacle courses have been constructed and tested, teams change over courses, and all members attempt to complete the course in turn. One person from each team will be needed to judge, and mark down penalty points for each fault. The game may be organised as a relay, with times recorded for all competitors, and seconds added on for the number of faults.

EQUIPMENT NEEDED FOR EACH TEAM: Pencil, paper, bamboo canes, string, scissors, large polythene sheet, wooden tent pegs, mallet, clip board, watch, blindfold.

MINI ASSAULT COURSE

THE PROBLEM: To design, and attempt to complete, a miniature assault course, using only the natural features which are already present. The area should ideally contain a grassy slope (not too steep!), a few large fallen trees, some trees with strong lower branches for climbing (not higher than say 8 ft.), and a few hollows or earth mounds. A typical course could include some of the following features: balance along a fallen tree, jump over a hollow, climb up a tree to about 8 ft., then move along a strong branch, drop down, run up the grassy slope, crawl through a hollow tree trunk, hop over some low earth mounds, snake under some low branches, and zig-zag through some trees to finish. The leader should check the course after it has been designed, and insist on changes, if necessary.

SAFETY: This exercise is meant to be an **EASY** version of an army assault course. The leader will need to lay down strict rules, to make clear the exact area to be used, the maximum height to be climbed, the maximum distance to jump, and any other specific safety points. All students should wear training shoes and old clothes. At least two adults are recommended for a maximum group size of ten. Be sure to choose a suitable area with public access.

FLYING MESSAGE

THE PROBLEM: To send a flying message (without throwing!) over a line which has been raised 12 feet above the ground. A suggested method is illustrated below.

STAGE 1.

A line is fixed between two trees or masts, at a height of 12 feet above ground level. A bow is made, and a long piece of string is attached to the arrow.

STAGE 2.

Following the leader's strict safety rules, the archer should aim to fire the arrow and string over the high line, and into a 6 foot diameter circle - which has been marked out on the grass. Part of the problem is to work out a method of keeping the string free from tangles as it runs out. A quick and easy method of retrieving the arrow and string (without using the bow), will also need to be considered.

TWANG

⟵ 15 FEET ⟶   ⟵ 15 FEET ⟶   ⟵ 6 FEET ⟶

MESSAGE

SAFETY LINE ⟶

STAGE 3. Only when the arrow lands inside the circle, can another member of the team move to the circle, and pull the string (with a message attached) over the high line and into the circle.

EQUIPMENT NEEDED FOR EACH TEAM: Overhead line, bendy stick for bow, smooth strait stick for arrow, long length of thin string (at least 50 feet), pen knife, small hacksaw, and message.

SAFETY: All members of the team (and spectators) should remain behind the safety line when the arrow is fired. If more than one team is engaged in the same exercise, then a safe distance between teams should be decided. One adult per team is recommended. Avoid areas with overhead power lines!

CANDLE LANTERNS

THE PROBLEM :   To design and construct a lantern, containing a candle, using only the equipment listed below. The lantern should be designed so that the lighted candle would not blow out in breezy conditions, and the shield would not catch fire. The final problem is to see which team can carry the lighted lantern, attached to the top of a long cane, for a distance of 50 metres out of doors.

EQUIPMENT NEEDED FOR EACH TEAM :   Pencil and paper, several short bamboo canes or garden canes, polythene sheet, scissors, string, tape, bendy wire, wire cutters, hacksaw, matches, candle, long bamboo cane.

STILES

THE PROBLEM: To design and construct a temporary stile over a fence or wall. This exercise provides opportunity for design, knot tying skills, and teamwork. Permission from the landowner may be required. Care should be taken to avoid any damage to the fence or wall.

Diagonal lashing used for the crossing point of the main poles.

Square lashing used to secure steps to main poles. The square lashing is finished with a reef knot.

Butt-ends may be dug in for additional security.

EQUIPMENT NEEDED FOR EACH TEAM: Strong wooden poles, of various length, strong lashing ropes, pencil and paper.

QUICK HAMMOCKS

THE PROBLEM : Session 1 - practise your knots on these quick hammocks. Session 2 - design and construct your own hammock or swing chair.

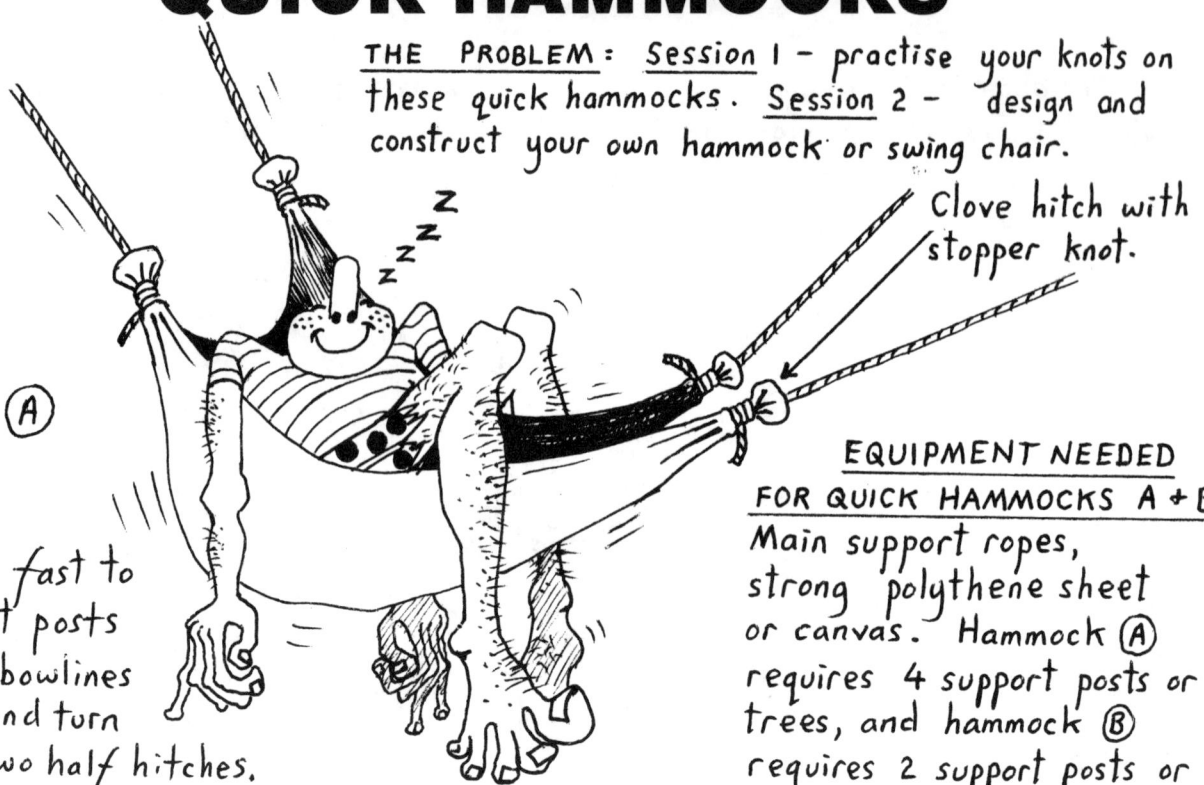

Clove hitch with stopper knot.

Ⓐ

Make fast to support posts with bowlines or round turn and two half hitches.

EQUIPMENT NEEDED

FOR QUICK HAMMOCKS A + B: Main support ropes, strong polythene sheet or canvas. Hammock Ⓐ requires 4 support posts or trees, and hammock Ⓑ requires 2 support posts or trees.

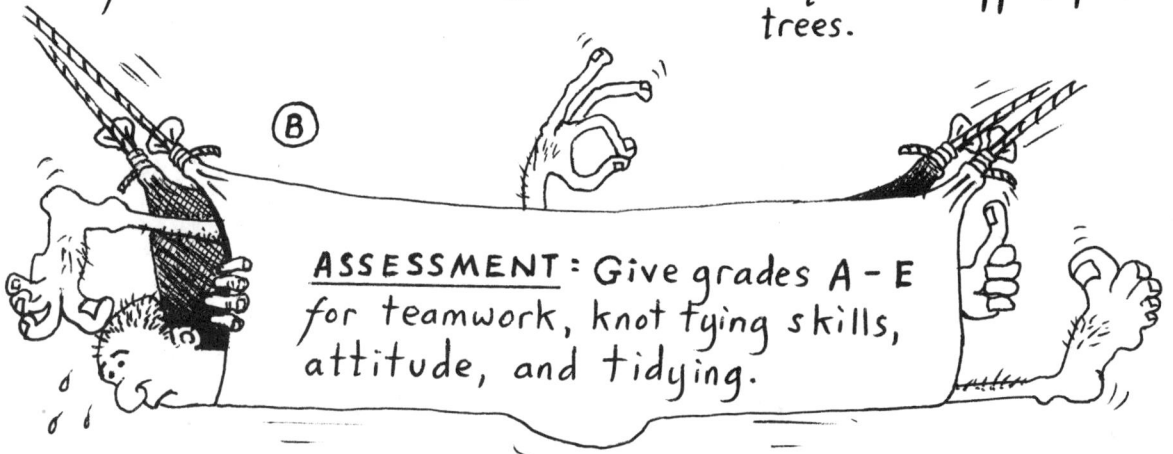

Ⓑ

ASSESSMENT : Give grades A - E for teamwork, knot tying skills, attitude, and tidying.

QUICK HAMMOCK Ⓒ : This method will probably take two students between one and two hours to construct. Equipment : main support ropes, strong lashing ropes for making net, and two wooden poles.

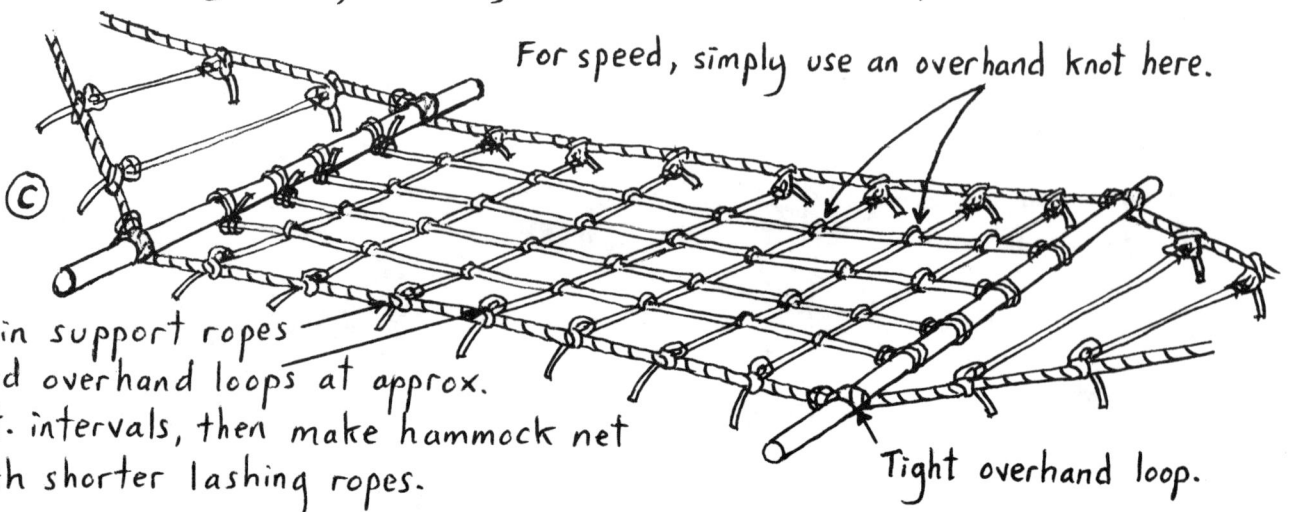

For speed, simply use an overhand knot here.

Ⓒ

Main support ropes need overhand loops at approx. 1 ft. intervals, then make hammock net with shorter lashing ropes.

Tight overhand loop.

SAFETY POINTS : No pushing !, Leader to check all knots and supports, Height - not more than 5 feet above the ground.

POTATO CONVEYOR

THE PROBLEM: To design and construct a structure for a potato (or tennis ball) to roll down, by gravity. The journey taken by the potato, should be as interesting as possible. There should be at least two main bends, and a drop, along the route. Points may be awarded for design, teamwork, practical skills, length of journey, and time in seconds for the journey, (the longest time gains the most points!).

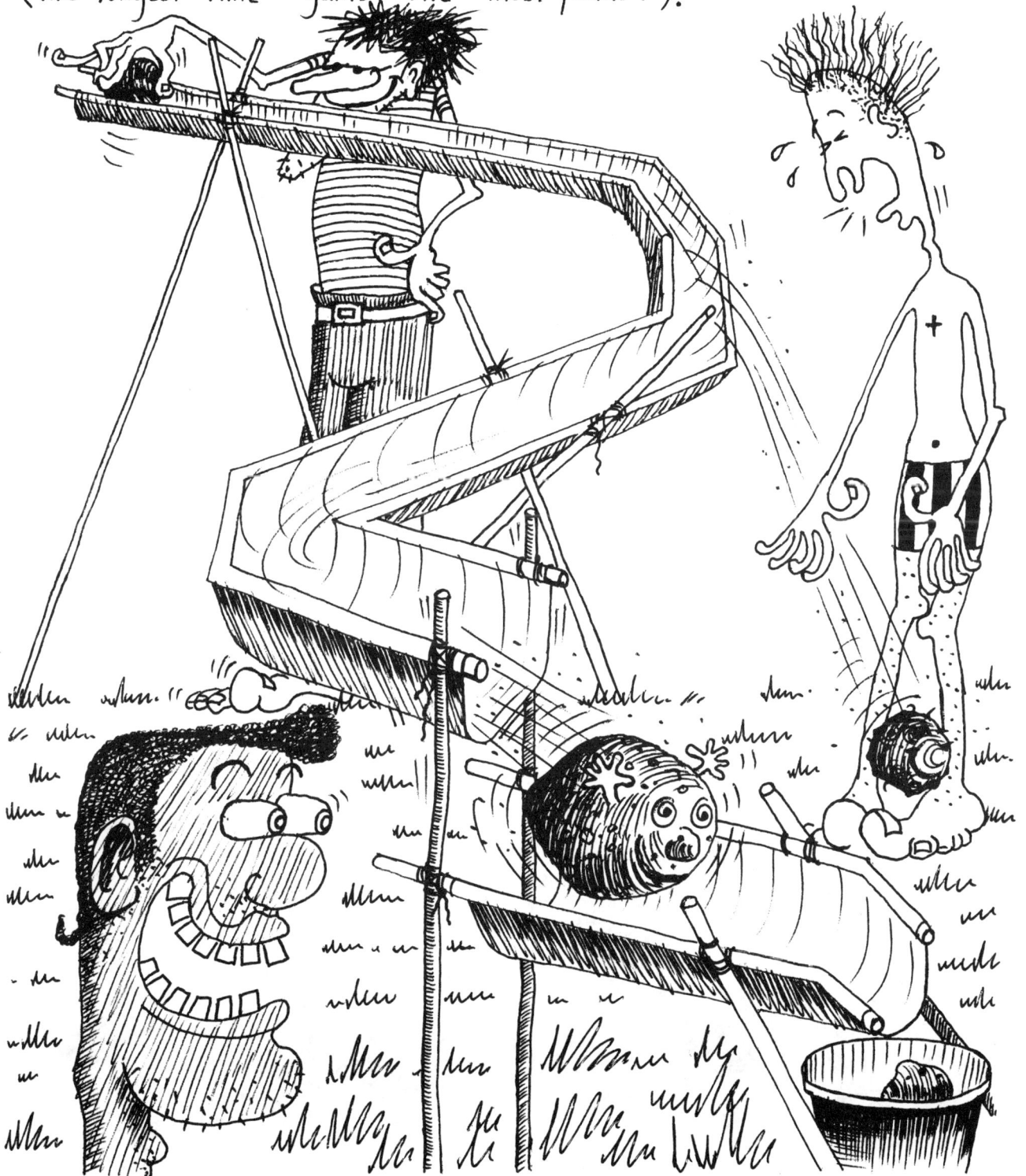

EQUIPMENT NEEDED FOR EACH TEAM: Pencil and paper, bamboo canes, hacksaw, strips of polythene, string, scissors, short length of tape, one round potato or tennis ball.

MODEL CARGO BOATS

THE PROBLEM: To design and construct a model boat, which should be stable enough to carry a given cargo. Each pair may choose one of the following types of boat to construct: catamaran, trimaran, canoe with outrigger, raft, coracle, cargo boat, punt. The maximum length of the model boat should be no more than one metre. Sails are optional.

A section of stream, preferably with a small rapid and a bend, should be chosen to test the finished models. Small plastic bags filled with sand or pebbles may be used for the cargo. The winning boat will be the one to carry the most cargo bags over the set distance, without capsizing.

EQUIPMENT: Pencil and paper, bamboo canes, bendy sticks, hacksaw, string, scissors, polythene sheet, small plastic containers (e.g. washing-up liquid type), tape, glue, various scraps of wood, cargo bags, long canes for rescuing drifting boats.

WATER TRANSPORTER

THE PROBLEM : To transport a bucket of water across a stream, at a height of 8 feet above the ground, using an overhead rope system. Each team must transport the suspended bucket of water along the overhead rope system, to the other side of the stream, without actually touching the bucket. The winning team will present their bucket, which contains the most water. <u>Note</u> : Protective wrapping should be used around trees on both sides of the stream.

EQUIPMENT NEEDED FOR EACH TEAM : Overhead rope, protective wrapping for trees, sisal twine, scissors, 1 large bucket, 1 small container (for filling the bucket, 1 karabiner.

SAFETY : This exercise is only intended for shallow streams, using only a bucket of water on the overhead rope system. The leader should check the security of the rope system, before the bucket is transported. Recommended knots for securing the overhead rope, are - bowlines, or, round turn and two half hitches.

SHADUF

A shaduf is a primitive method of raising water from a river to irrigation ditches. The structure, using poles and bucket, has been used for centuries in Egypt, along the banks of the River Nile.

THE PROBLEM: To design and construct a shaduf. The structure will be free-standing, using a tripod or similar method, and the bucket will be attached to a long pole which pivots at the apex of the tripod. By applying weight to the long pole, the bucket (or container) may be raised, lowered, or moved from side to side.

The final problem, which is best done as a team race, is to see how much water can be raised from a stream or river, and tipped into another bucket on the bank side, in a time of say 3 minutes.

EQUIPMENT NEEDED FOR EACH TEAM:

6 x7 ft. poles, lengths of lashing rope, ball of string, scissors, 1 large-bucket, and 1 small bucket or container.

CARRY SEATS

THE PROBLEM: To design and construct a contraption with a seat, for carrying a person. The finished product should be safe for the passenger, even when transported in a carry seat race! This exercise is intended for teams of 5 people.

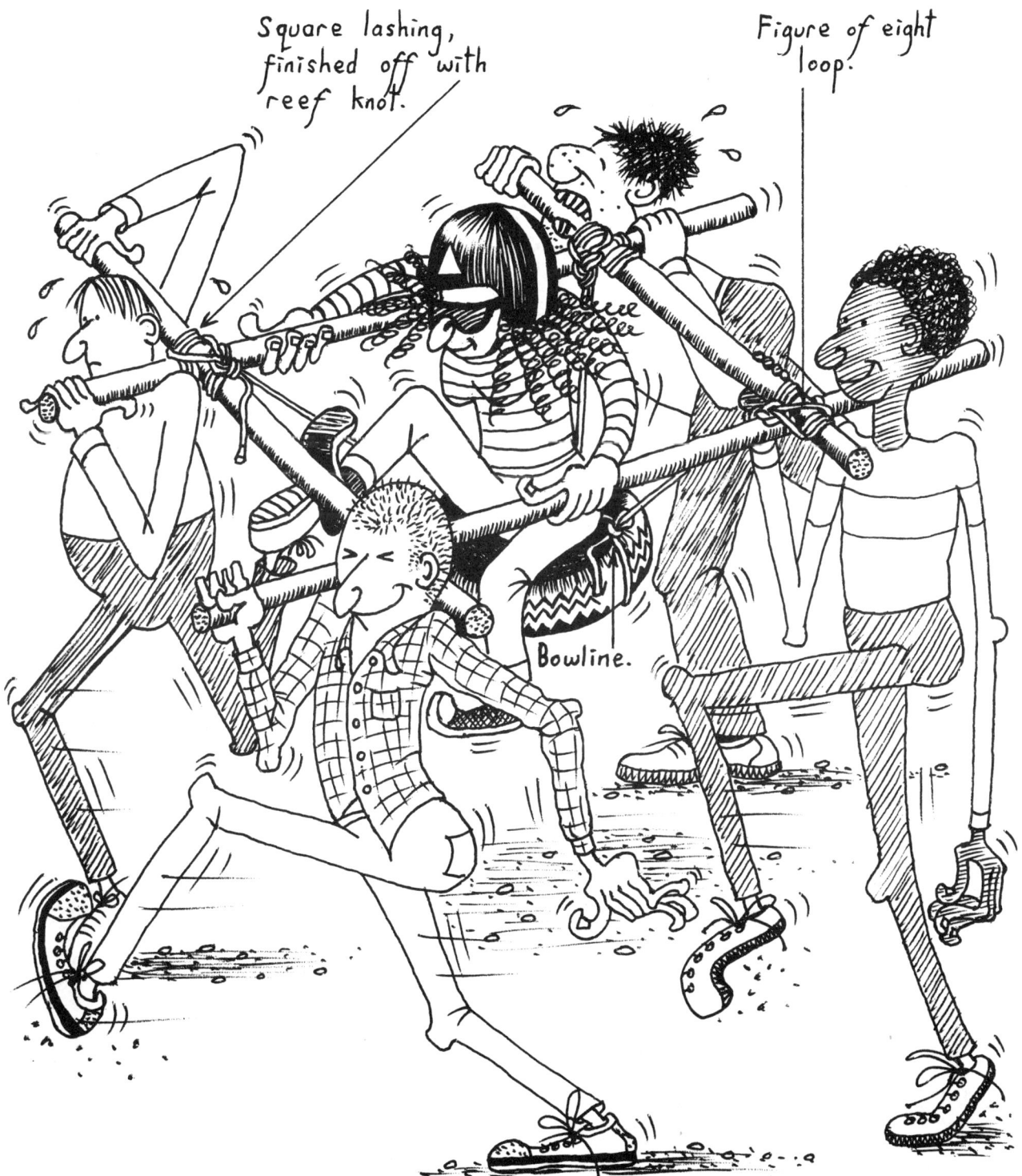

Square lashing, finished off with reef knot.

Figure of eight loop.

Bowline.

EQUIPMENT NEEDED FOR EACH TEAM: 4 strong wooden poles for the frame, strong lashing ropes, old car tyre, crash helmet (optional).

SIGN POST

THE PROBLEM : To design and construct a sign post, which should point to a number of places marked on the map. This may be done at a suitable point during a walk, or in the grounds at the base. The leader may divide the group into teams, and give instructions to build a sign post, using dead sticks from the surrounding area. The completed sign post should point accurately to at least ten villages, or places of interest, and give clear indication of place names, compass directions (e.g. N.E.), and direct distance in kilometres.

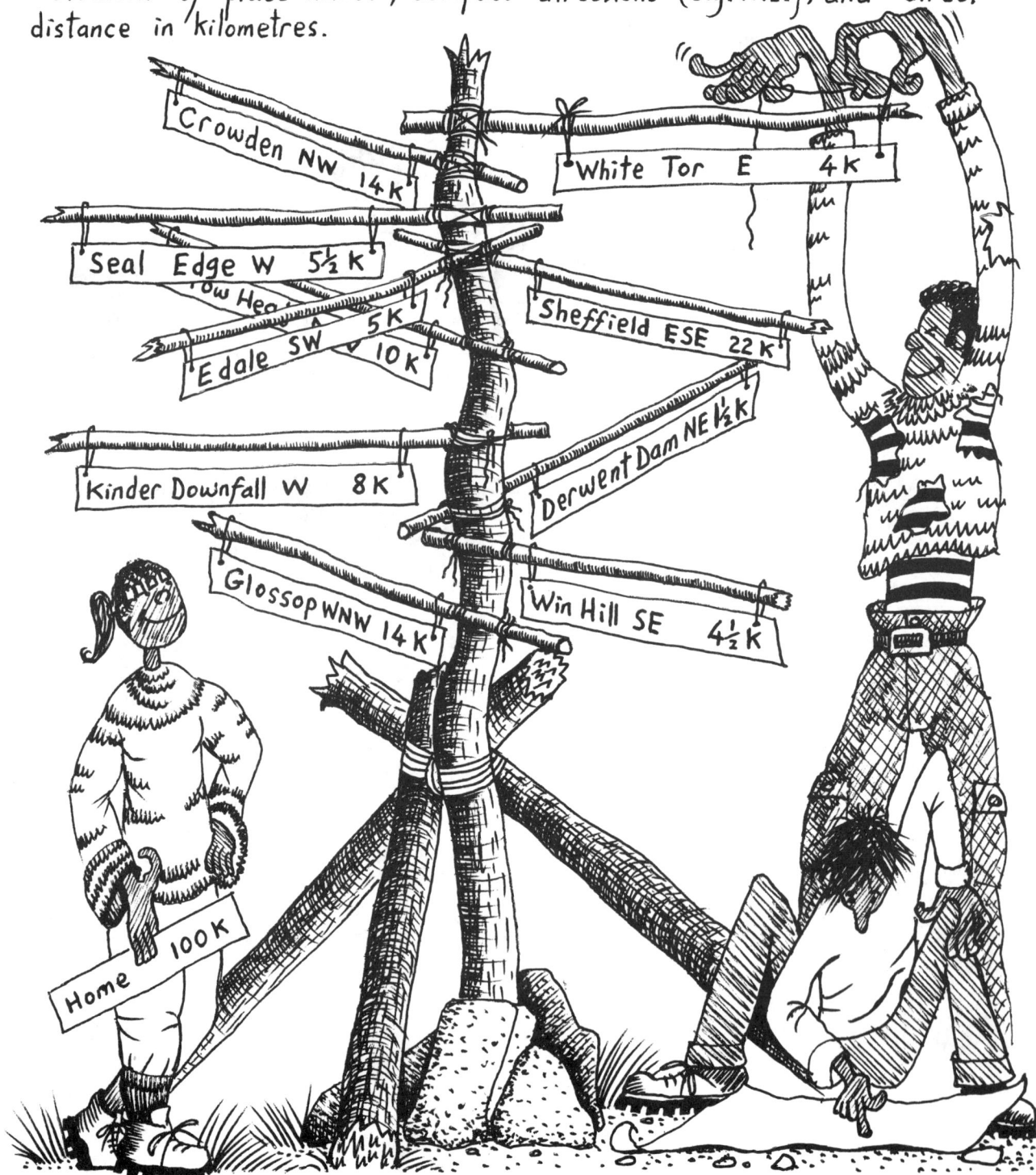

Crowden NW 14 k

White Tor E 4 k

Seal Edge W 5½ k

Row Head

Sheffield ESE 22 k

Edale SW 5 k 10 k

Derwent Dam NE 1½ k

Kinder Downfall W 8 K

Glossop WNW 14 k

Win Hill SE 4½ K

Home 100 K

EQUIPMENT NEEDED FOR EACH TEAM : Dead sticks, string or sisal twine, cardboard strips, scissors, marker pens, Ordnance Survey map, compass, and camera if possible, to record the team at work and the finished product.

BRICKHENGE

THE PROBLEM: To apply fundamental moving and lifting principles, to construct a miniature **Stonehenge**, using bricks. The idea is to build the model, using labour saving devices, as shown in the sketches below. The bricks should not be touched by hand at any stage of the exercise.

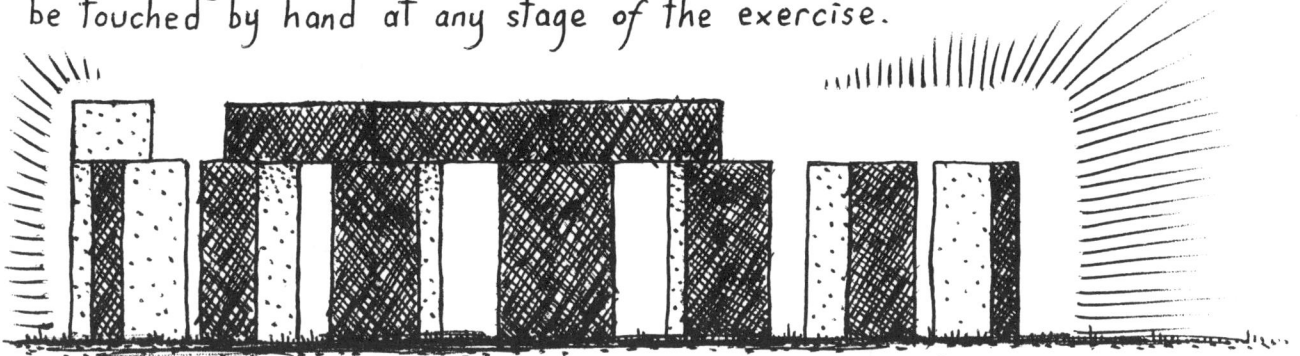

STAGE 1. Mark out a semicircle (radius 1 metre) on the ground, to represent only the eastern half of the existing Stonehenge Sarsen Circle. The approximate positions of 17 standing bricks (numbered), and 7 brick lintels (▭), are shown in the sketch plan opposite.

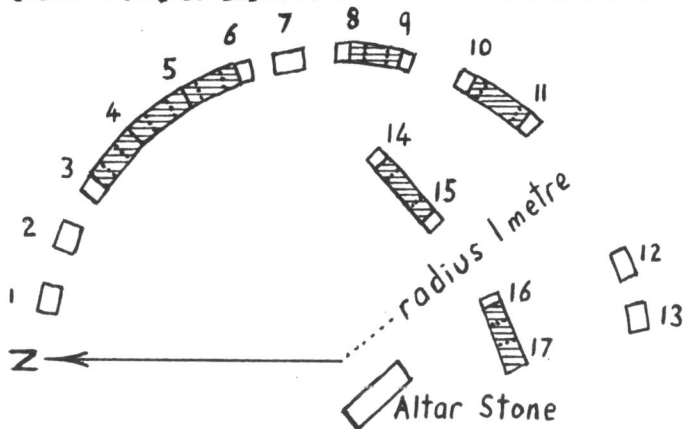

STAGE 2. The bricks may be moved into position on cane rollers, using thin string for pulling, and thin sticks for pushing or manoeuvring.

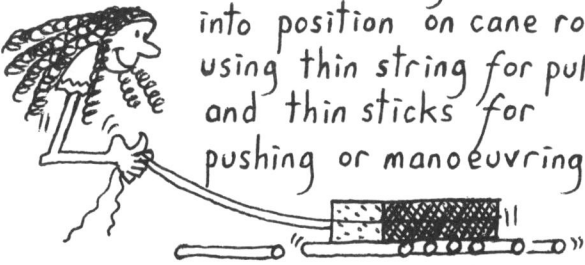

STAGE 3.

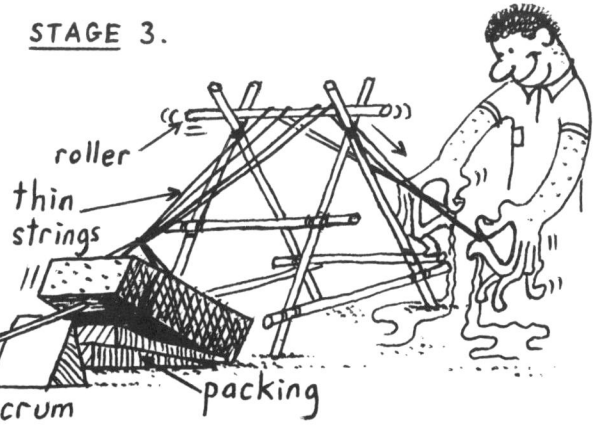

roller
thin strings
fulcrum   packing

STAGE 4.

long lever

(stage 3 continued) Each brick should be lifted into its upright position, by using a thin stick as a long lever, to raise the brick a few millimetres at a time. Packing is pushed underneath the brick each time it is raised. A wooden structure may be built, so that thin strings may be used to lightly pull or lower. Depending on the ground surface, holes may be dug for the base of the bricks to rest in.

(stage 4 continued) The upright bricks may then be buried in sand or earth, and a wooden ramp layed down, so that the brick lintels may be gently pulled into their final positions.

NOTE: The methods used in this exercise are not necessarily the same methods used in the actual construction of Stonehenge.

ALL NIGHT PROBLEMS

This demanding exercise is intended for senior students who have had some experience of orienteering, map and compass training, and camp crafts. Even with an experienced group, it would be necessary to hold a number of planning and training meetings with all of the students.

The idea of this exercise, is for teams of 2 or 3 students to navigate through the night, in fairly mild countryside, on public paths, bridleways, and minor roads. A number of problems are set at various points throughout the route. The teams attempt to solve each problem, and finally navigate to a finish point, where an improvised shelter is to be set up to sleep in.

The 'night navigation' page, in chapter one, gives a suggested outline, which may be amended to fit your particular objectives.

A piece of advice for leaders thinking of tackling this exercise, is to make sure you have plenty of willing helpers, who are prepared to put up with a full night without sleep!

<u>PROCEDURE</u>: ① The teams are timed out at intervals of about 5 minutes, (after an equipment check).

② The teams navigate to a number of orienteering markers which are set out along the route.

③ The teams check in at a few manned controls, and show their control cards.

④ The teams must solve a few problems, at set points along the route; e.g. using a given code system, found in an envelope at a check point, use a torch to flash a coded message (to identify the name of your group?), and receive a coded message, which will be flashed back.

⑤ At the finish point, the teams must construct a shelter to sleep in, using the materials provided. Boys sleep in separate shelters to the girls. A meal is to be cooked, on a stove, or open fire, depending on the location, and experience of the group.

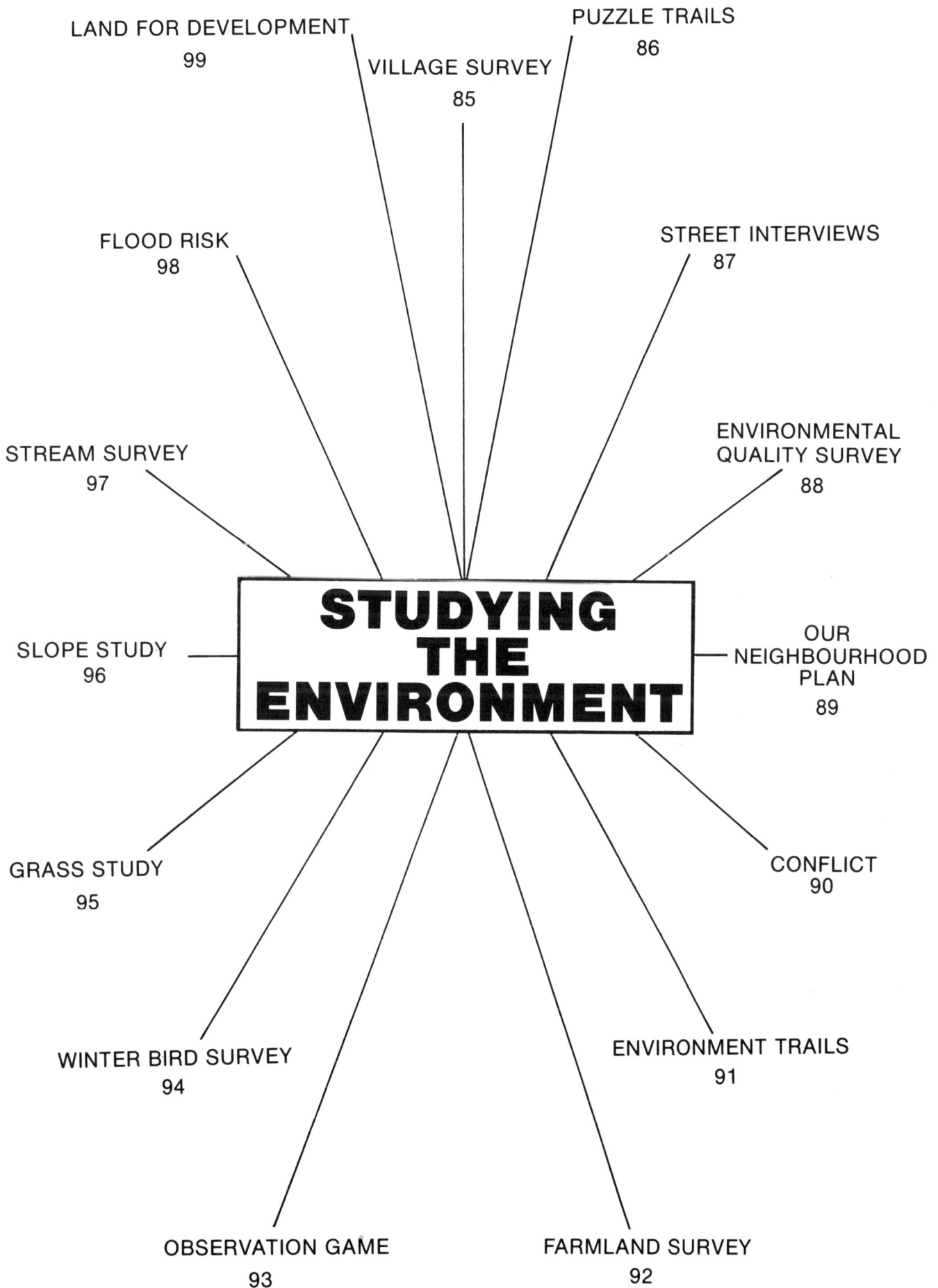

CHAPTER FIVE

LAND FOR DEVELOPMENT
99

PUZZLE TRAILS
86

VILLAGE SURVEY
85

STREET INTERVIEWS
87

FLOOD RISK
98

STREAM SURVEY
97

ENVIRONMENTAL
QUALITY SURVEY
88

STUDYING THE ENVIRONMENT

SLOPE STUDY
96

OUR
NEIGHBOURHOOD
PLAN
89

GRASS STUDY
95

CONFLICT
90

WINTER BIRD SURVEY
94

ENVIRONMENT TRAILS
91

OBSERVATION GAME
93

FARMLAND SURVEY
92

STUDYING THE ENVIRONMENT

By studying the environment through a variety of surveys and exercises in the field, an appreciation of our rural and urban landscapes can be developed.

The exercises in this chapter are presented at quite a basic level. They are intended for anyone with an interest in their environment, and background knowledge of the particular subjects should not be necessary. It is anticipated, however, that some of the ideas here may be developed into more detailed investigations, including GCSE assessment projects.

The pages here attempt to show a range of possibilities for looking at the environment with small groups of young people. The cartoons illustrate various methods of recording observations, measuring and estimating distances, and using basic communicating skills. Hopefully these exercises are designed so that the work will be interesting and enjoyable. Maximum individual involvement is essential. To encourage this, the group may be divided into pairs of students, each pair with responsibility for completing a number of tasks. The adult leader or teacher should always be fairly close at hand to give help and encouragement, and to offer guidance.

All students involved in environmental studies should be fully aware of the Country Code. The 'CONFLICT' exercise in this chapter will help students to understand some of the implications of the Country Code.

A selection of follow up exercises has been included at the bottom of most pages in this chapter. They may offer some ideas for developing the work done in the field.

Books and resources which I have found particularly useful are : 'Exploring the Environment' by Roger Clare (published by Macdonald); 'Discovering Derbyshire (1)' edited by Harry Tolley (published by The University of Nottingham School of Education); 'Observer Pocket Series', especially useful in this chapter for identifying grasses, birds, trees and buildings (architecture); and Ordnance Survey maps which are always an important resource for people involved in environmental studies.

Acknowledgement: The idea for the 'LAND FOR DEVELOPMENT' exercise on page 99 is based on a set of Geography teaching materials produced by the Schools Council Development Project Team.

VILLAGE SURVEY

The aim of this survey is to make simple labelled sketches, to show the shape, character and use of buildings along a given frontage.
The group may be split up into pairs, so that sketches may be made of all the interesting parts of the village.

Back at the base, a cardboard stand up model could be made by cutting out the skyline shapes of the buildings and adding as much colour and detail as possible to capture the real character of the village. The finished model may then form the basis for further investigations, e.g. land use patterns, conservation areas, traffic problem areas, building structures, etc.

VALUE :

(stand up model)

environmental awareness
aesthetic appreciation
concentration
self discipline
field sketching skills
annotating skills

HIGH STREET

PUZZLE TRAILS

Puzzle trails are especially suitable for village and town studies. They may be organised in 'street orienteering' style as outlined in chapter two. The students will need a map and a list of puzzles to solve. A selection of possible puzzle questions is given below.

① <u>Sign post</u>
The letters in this town have been jumbled :

> ROBGGHOLUUO 7 >

Answer : _ _ _ _ _ _ _ _ _ _

② <u>Old school tower</u>
Which silhouette shape is correct ?

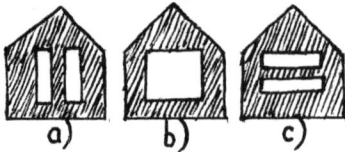

a)   b)   c)

③ <u>Corner shop sign</u>
Look at the reflections.

a) ЯƎHϽTUB
b) ЯƎϽOЯG
c) TИƎGASWƎИ

Correct answer : _ _ _ _ _ _ _ _

④ <u>Church gate</u>
Circle the five mistakes that have been shown on the gate below.

⑤ <u>Old thatched cottage</u>
How old is the cottage ?
(Subtract the date of the cottage from this year.)
Answer : _ _ _ _ years .

⑥ <u>Road junction</u>
Which map shows the correct positions of the church (⛪) and post office (P)?

a)   b)   c)

⑦ <u>Monument</u>
Complete the missing details.

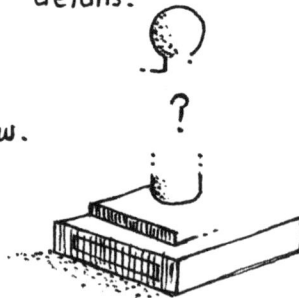

?

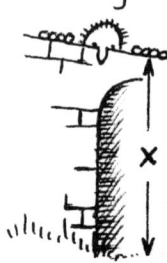

⑧ <u>Bridge</u>
Estimate the <u>height</u> of the bridge at X.
Assume that each stone block is 40 cm high.
Number of blocks = _ _ _
Total height at X = _ _ _

⑨ <u>Main Street</u>
Find the names of the three hotels on Main Street in the wordsearch below.

A	L	N	E	P	T	A	J	C	I
D	V	I	D	T	O	B	I	N	B
O	H	R	J	H	G	E	N	W	H
G	L	O	R	E	M	N	O	K	N
A	V	B	T	F	S	R	I	G	N
N	F	I	U	I	C	P	L	M	I
D	D	A	B	S	D	B	D	S	W
G	A	M	E	H	O	T	E	L	E
U	I	O	Q	W	K	U	R	C	N
N	D	A	E	H	S	L	L	U	B

⑩ <u>Car Park</u>
Which of the following route(s) is/are possible by car ?

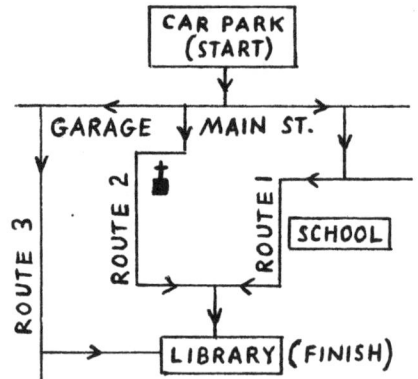

CAR PARK (START)
GARAGE   MAIN ST.
ROUTE 3   ROUTE 2   ROUTE 1   SCHOOL
LIBRARY (FINISH)

⑪ <u>Church Street</u>
Write **TRUE** or **FALSE** if you can find these buildings on Church St.

NEWSAGENT _ _ _ _ _
HOTEL _ _ _ _ _
CAFE _ _ _ _
POST OFFICE _ _ _ _
RECTORY _ _ _ _ _

As the students often enjoy making up their own puzzles, they could add five more puzzle questions to the list as they walk around the trail, and number them on their street map.

STREET INTERVIEWS

An interesting way of collecting information for a local study is to go out into the community with a set of questions that have been worked out in advance. This method of interviewing people in the street provides an unusual and exciting approach for the students who will probably gain much from the experience, if it is done correctly.

The questions could be set to find out about people's shopping habits; about local problems such as traffic or pollution; or about local attitudes to new developments such as a new mine or factory.

'Excuse me, we are from North Street school; do you mind if we ask you a few questions............?'

VALUE :
communication with adults
self awareness
self confidence
responsibilities
personal conduct
situation experience
environmental awareness

SOME SUGGESTIONS : Students should always be polite, even when people do not want to be interviewed. The questionnaire should be easy to use outside; this could mean having questions with short alternative answers to tick. The students may be involved in designing the questionnaire. Students should be given a definite area to work in. This is best done alone or in pairs, but never more than two. A tape recorder may be used, especially if longer answers or opinions are required. Be careful not to overuse this method in the same area. Alternative surveys should be ready for students who show signs that they can not cope with the situation.

FOLLOW UP WORK : 1) Compare results with other students doing the same survey. 2) Draw up the results of the surveys in the form of maps, graphs or diagrams, and make some conclusions.

ENVIRONMENTAL QUALITY SURVEY

The aim of this survey is to compare the environmental quality in three different areas.

'My grandad wouldn't like to live there!'

NORTH END FLATS

VICTORIA ST

'These old terraced houses have been well looked after!'

'I wonder if my Dad's at home?'

PASTURES LANE

Name of Street: North End Flats	Names: Jill and Wayne.

Show your opinion of the environmental quality of this street by shading the boxes below

Factors	HIGH QUALITY ⟷ LOW	Factors	HIGH QUALITY ⟷ LOW
State of repair		Greenery (e.g. trees)	
Character of buildings		Surrounding land use	
View from windows		Traffic (safe ⟷ dangerous)	
Daylight through windows		Street lighting	
House entrance designs		Outside noise level	
Car space		Air cleanliness	
Vandalism (lack of ⟷ much)		Shop access	
Privacy		Public transport (e.g. bus stops)	
Garden size		Pavements	
Neighbourhood play areas		Other (specify): Entertainment	

FOLLOW UP WORK: 1) Rewrite the list of 20 factors in your order of importance.
2) Draw suitable graphs or diagrams to show the results of your survey.
3) Write a letter to your local council, suggesting realistic ways of improving the environment in your survey area.

NOTE: Be careful not to overuse this survey in the same streets.

OUR NEIGHBOURHOOD PLAN

The aim of this exercise is to design a new neighbourhood centre for one hundred years ahead. The new centre would be based on the site of the existing centre, and may retain some of the chosen existing features. The students should already be familiar with the functions of a neighbourhood centre with its transport systems and services.

STAGE ① A visit to the site will need to be arranged, for the group to make a plan showing the existing layout and use of buildings, roads and other special features. Each pair of students will need a large scale base map of the road system, onto which notes and symbols are to be added.

STAGE ② DESIGNING AND MAKING THE NEIGHBOURHOOD PLAN :
Different coloured pieces of card may be cut to shape, labelled and positioned on the base map (see below), to show the new neighbourhood centre design. Card may be used to give a 3D effect for some features, e.g. flyovers, high level transport systems, and particular buildings.

TEAM ASSESSMENT	
FIELDWORK ROUGH PLANS	20
FIELDWORK EFFORT	20
DESIGN AND ORIGINALITY	20
FINISHED PRODUCT	20
ORAL PRESENTATION	20
TOTAL POINTS	100

STAGE ③ Each team should be prepared to talk about their plan to the whole group. This would involve pointing out the main features, giving reasons for aspects of the design, and defending their plans against opposition from critics.

CONFLICT

Simulate a situation where a small group of hikers meet up with a landowner. This may be done in several different ways, e.g. 1) The bad mannered hikers have gone the wrong way across the landowner's field, and both sides exchange their strong opinions, with the hikers eventually continuing undeterred along their illegal route; 2) The polite group of hikers has gone the correct way across the landowner's field, but the angry landowner turns them back; 3) The polite group of hikers has gone the correct way across the landowner's field. They meet up with the landowner, and both sides sensibly and calmly exchange their views.

NOTE: Students involved in acting out this situation should show SELF CONTROL and RESTRAINT.

CONCLUSIONS:
What should be the best way to behave in these situations?
What reasons may the landowner give for turning you off his land?
What polite answers may the hikers give to the landowner?
What would happen if all hikers took no notice of fences, paths and signs?
NOTE: A useful section on access is included in Eric Langmuir's 'Mountaincraft and Leadership'.

ENVIRONMENT TRAILS

Environment trails can be worked out on questionnaire style sheets. A set route marked on a sketch map will be required for the students to follow.

Various questions are completed and observations made en route. These could be related to a variety of environmental features, e.g. land use, building styles, map features, plants, land shape, geological features, special features, e.g. bridge, dam, wall, lock gate, waterfall. Choose a variety of things to do, to prevent the questions from becoming repetitive.

POINT ①
(first field)
What does the farmer use this field for?
(5 points)

POINT ② (old stone barn)
Estimate the area of the barn.

length ___ metres x width ___ m
= _____ square metres. (15 points)

POINT ③ (path junction)
Use your Ordnance Survey map to find out where the 4 paths lead to. (20 points)

POINT ⑤ (ancient burial mounds)
Make a simple sketch map of the burial mounds, using the symbols provided. (50 points)

RATTLE!

POINT ④
(plantation corner)
Sketch the leaves of 2 different conifer trees, and collect a cone from the ground for your display.

TOTAL POINTS

OUT OF 200

The style of questions or tasks in the field should be designed to allow maximum individual involvement. Small groups or pairs working on their own should be encouraged when possible. The role of the leader here should be as a guide who gives suggestions and encouragement, but at the same time allows the students to think and work things out for themselves.

FARMLAND SURVEY

As the students walk along a country lane or track, they may observe the land use on either side of them, and record symbols to make up a simple map. Symbols may also be added to show estimated quality of farmland and type of livestock. A pocket reference book would be useful for students to identify the different types of crops and animals.

Some farmland symbols:

ARABLE
barley (b)
wheat (w)
oats (o)
oilseed rape (r)
potatoes (p)
sugar beet (sb)
swedes (s)

Other symbols:
deciduous wood (♣ ♣ ♣)
coniferous wood (↟ ↟ ↟)
fallow (f)
marsh (ᵕᵕᵕ)

GRASS
permanent pasture (pp)
rough pasture (rp)
ley (l)

Livestock symbols:

CATTLE
Friesian (F)
Hereford (H)
Charollais (C)
Ayrshire (A)
Highland (Hi)

SHEEP
Derbyshire Gritstone (DG)
Swaledale (Sw)
Scottish Blackface (SB).

Before the survey, a land quality scale may be worked out together, e.g. ranging from flat, fertile land = 10 to steep, rocky land = 1

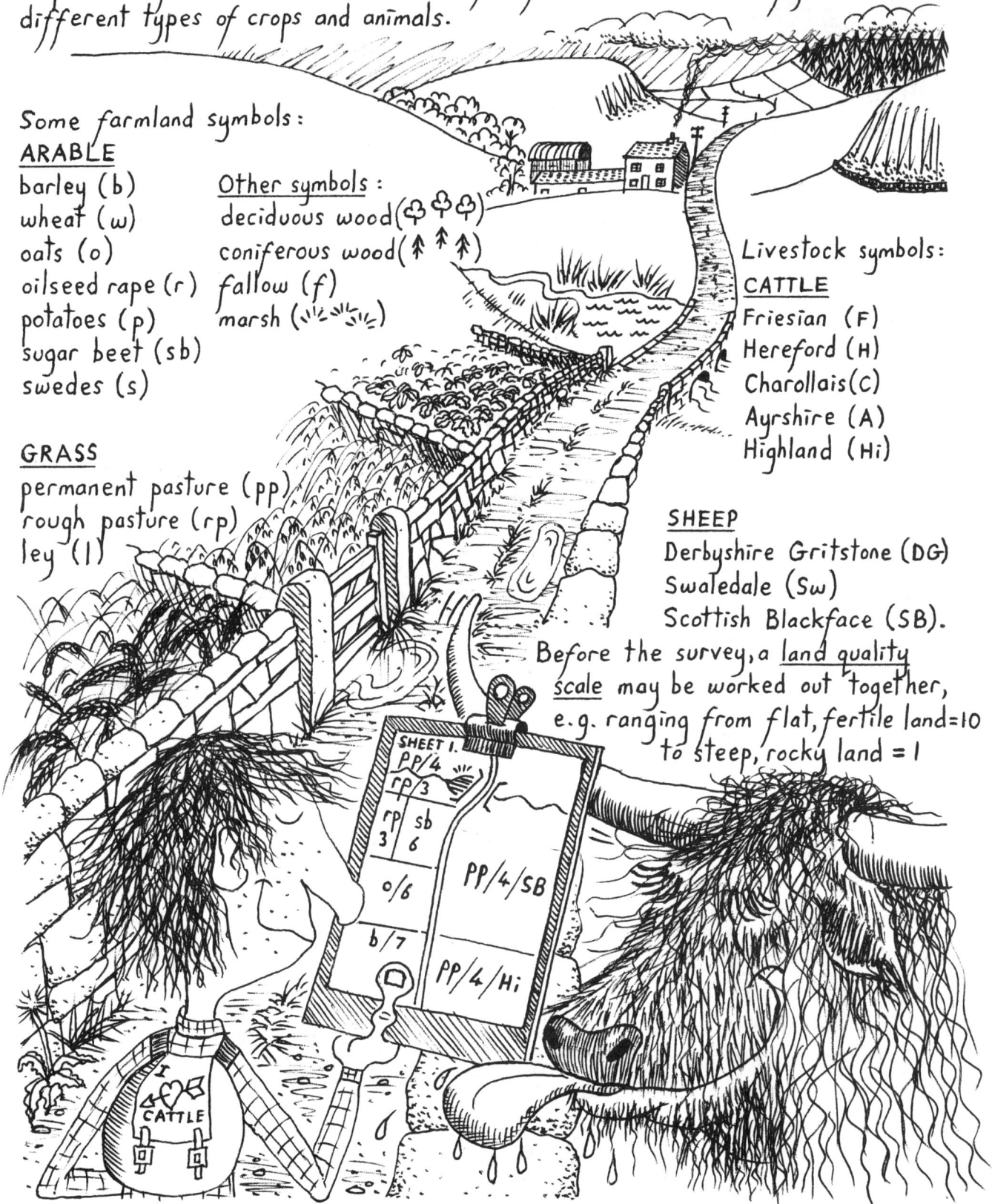

SHEET 1.
PP/4
rp/3
rp 3 sb 6
o/6
b/7
PP/4/SB
PP/4/Hi

CATTLE

The farmer's permission may be needed for this survey.
FOLLOW UP WORK: 1) Draw up your land use map using colour and symbols.
2) Try to explain why the farmer has used his fields in this way.
3) Comment on the problems for farming in your survey area.

OBSERVATION GAME

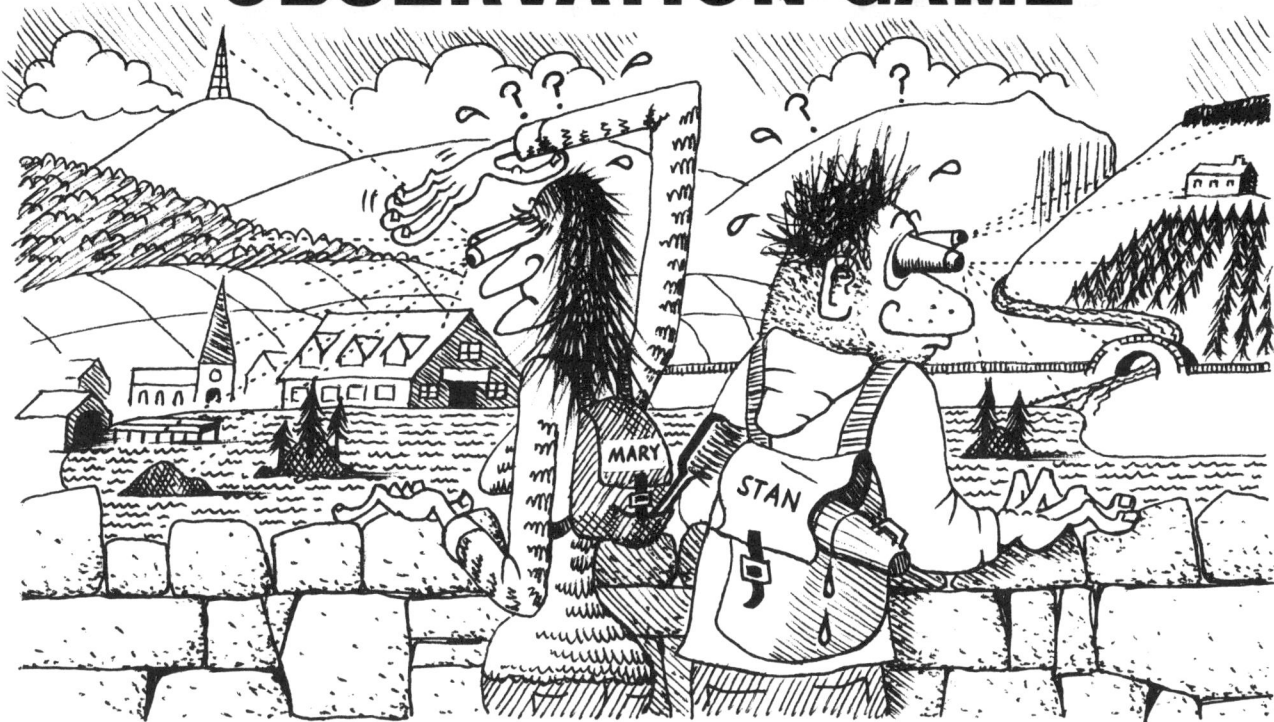

'O.K. Mary and Stan, you are on a spying mission in enemy territory, and you have sixty seconds to use your photographic memories'.

The students are expected to remember as much detail as possible about the view, which may be a panoramic landscape, a village, a farm, or an interesting building. If possible the chosen points for the observation game should be pre planned, so the view is hidden as the students approach.

There are several different ways of doing this exercise, depending on the level of difficulty required.

<u>Easiest method</u> : The students observe and then answer questions orally.

<u>Medium method</u> : The students observe and then tick off a simple check list.

<u>Hard method</u> : The students observe and then make a fully labelled sketch from memory.

<u>What to look for</u> :   (position of church ?)   (largest building ?)   (shape of wood?)

(feature on hill top ?)   (direction of road ?)   (position of river estuary?)

(number of islands ?)   (colour of hotel ?)   (size of village ?)

(position of pier ?)   (large industrial feature on hillside ?)   (type of bridge ?)

(estimated length of lake ?)   (pattern of fields ?)   (other observations?)

NOTE : Students would not be expected to do this observation game without some preliminary guidelines, clues and examples.

WINTER BIRD SURVEY

A frozen park lake presents an ideal opportunity for close range birdwatching. A bag full of crumbs will make the outing even more rewarding, as many wild ducks, geese and swans will readily accept food at very close range when they are hungry. A simple survey can be carried out along a set route, which passes through a variety of habitats. The survey is likely to be more successful if all members of the group are shown pictures of the likely birds to be seen, at the start of the route.

DANGER : DO NOT WALK ON THE ICE !

PARK LAKE BIRD SURVEY

As you walk around the route, record the symbols on the map to show exactly where you observed each species of bird. Also record the approx. numbers seen (ⅢⅢ = 5).

N W E S

CAR PARK

r

cr

bt

c cg m ms starlings 12

c c gg

mh cg c

wp c gcg

th LAKE c

bg mh cg c m cr bt

mp c c ms

m

0 100 metres

owl

EACH SYMBOL ON THE MAP MAY SHOW A GROUP OF BIRDS

Name(s) Jason, Jill + Jim.	Date	1ST Feb.
Weather conditions −1°c, snow showers		

BIRDS and SYMBOLS	NUMBERS	TOTAL
mallard (m)	ⅢⅢ ⅢⅠ	9
mute swan (ms)	ⅢⅠ	4
canada goose (cg)	ⅢⅢ ⅢⅢ ⅢⅢ ⅢⅢ ⅢⅢ	25
black headed gull (bg)	ⅢⅢ ⅢⅢ ⅢⅢ	15
grey lag goose (gg)	ⅠⅠ	2
coot (c)	ⅢⅢ ⅢⅢ ⅢⅢ ⅢⅢ	20
moorhen (mh)	ⅢⅠ	3
great crested grebe (gcg)	ⅠⅠ	2
crow (cr)	ⅢⅠ	3
song thrush (th)	ⅠⅠ	2
blue tit (bt)	ⅢⅠ	4
robin (r)	Ⅰ	1
wood pigeon (p)	ⅢⅢ Ⅰ	6
magpie (mp)	ⅢⅠ	3

FOLLOW UP WORK: Draw two labelled bar graphs, i) to show the number of each species of bird observed, and ii) to show which birds come close to humans and which birds keep a safe distance. Compare the two graphs.

GRASS STUDY

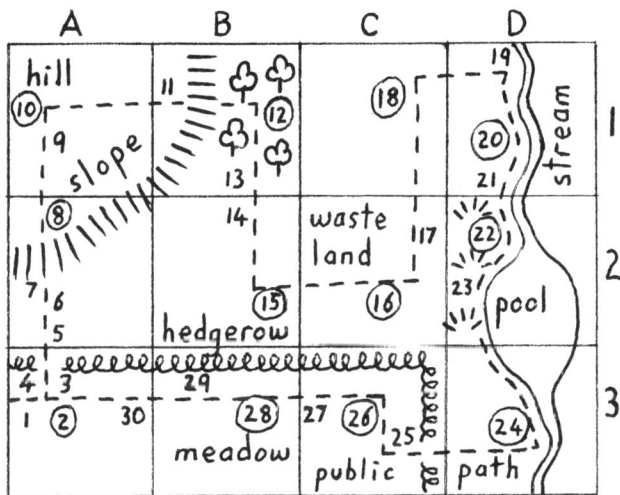

Grid map to show how the different specimens may be recorded in the field. The numbers may be circled on the map to show the most common grass in each grid square. The survey area should include a variety of different environments.

Before the survey, the students may make their own display wallets from cardboard. This will help to keep the specimens in order as they are collected, as the pockets are numbered according to the map grids.
A magnifying lense would be useful for close investigation of the specimens, and for identification using a suitable reference book (e.g. THE OBSERVER'S BOOK OF GRASSES, SEDGES & RUSHES).

This can be a very pleasant and interesting survey to do in early summer when a variety of grassheads are fully formed. The students may be given a grid map of the survey area, and their job is to collect as many different types of grass seed heads as possible, and number each different specimen on the grid map. To add a little competition to the exercise, 10 points may be awarded for each different species collected, and 50 points for a species that no one else has found.

(Home made display wallet)

SLOPE STUDY

Suitable footwear will be needed for this study. Only safe slopes should be used. A sketch section of the slope would be useful for the students to record their observations.

FOLLOW UP WORK : Make a cardboard model of the slope, with labels, measurements, and samples attached to show changes in vegetation, soils, geology, land use and wild life.

STREAM SURVEY

Each team is given a section of stream to survey and map. If possible, a clean, safe stream should be chosen with a variety of interesting features. This exercise tends to be more popular in the summer months when the students can paddle around without suffering from cold. Quite an accurate map can be drawn using pace counting or measuring tape for linear distances, and a long cane marked in centimetres for measuring the depth of water at selected points.

'The distance between X and Y is 2 paces'

'The depth here is 40 cm'

'The height of the stream cliff is 222 cm'

The following symbols may be shown on a sketch map of the stream:

fine particles deposited

larger pebbles and stones (2cm to 6cm)

large boulders

Use labels for bankside vegetation

shows position of rapids or small waterfalls

deep water

shallow water

2 → linear distance in metres

40 = sample depth in cm

fast current

slower current

steep bank slope

////// moderate bank slope

222 sample height of bank in cm

FOLLOW UP WORK: 1) Make a neat copy of your stream survey map, complete with symbols, key, measurements, labels, colour and date.
2) After a heavy rain storm and flood, it is possible that the appearance of your section of stream could change completely. On an outline of your section of stream, attempt to show how the symbols, measurements and labels could change. Give an explanation.

FLOOD RISK

The group may be divided into teams with responsibility for measuring and recording characteristics of the stream and its channel at several points.
This survey is mainly intended for lowland streams, where any major rise in water level could result in flood damage to the surrounding area. The survey should only be done when the stream is at a safe level for fieldwork.

width = 12 metres

90°

'Hm, the width of the stream is 12 metres, so if discharge = velocity × depth × width, then the discharge today is 2 × 0·5 × 12 = 12 cubic metres per second'.

45°

PROTRACTOR

12 metres

'The average velocity at this point is 2 metres per second'.

'This bank will be eroded away soon!'

10 metres

'The average depth of water is 0·5 metres, so only a rise of 1·5 metres and the school will be flooded!'

SCHOOL

FOLLOW UP WORK:
1) Draw a map of the stream you have studied, and shade blue the area that would be flooded if the stream breached its banks.
2) Make a list of the buildings, roads and land that would be flooded.
3) Calculate the maximum discharge of the stream (at the same recorded velocity) without flooding.

'I hope it rains tonight!'

SCHOOL

CLOSED

LAND FOR DEVELOPMENT

It is likely that somewhere near to your home, plans have been made for a major development which could dramatically affect your environment. Such a development could be a new road, a new factory, a new hypermarket, a new mine, or a new housing estate. This exercise suggests a possible method of investigating a new mining development.

STAGE ① A field visit may be arranged to make notes and sketches, and to take photographs of the site. These would be useful to help build up opinions about the character and quality of the area.

NEW MINE SITE

STAGE ② In preparation for a public inquiry (role play exercise), each student would need to decide which of the characters he or she is going to be. Preparation notes should then be made.

STAGE ③ THE PUBLIC INQUIRY (role play exercise)
An appointed chairman would introduce the speakers, give reasons for the public inquiry, and give a final summary. Each spokesperson may have an adviser. Speakers should be prepared to state their case and defend their case if questioned.

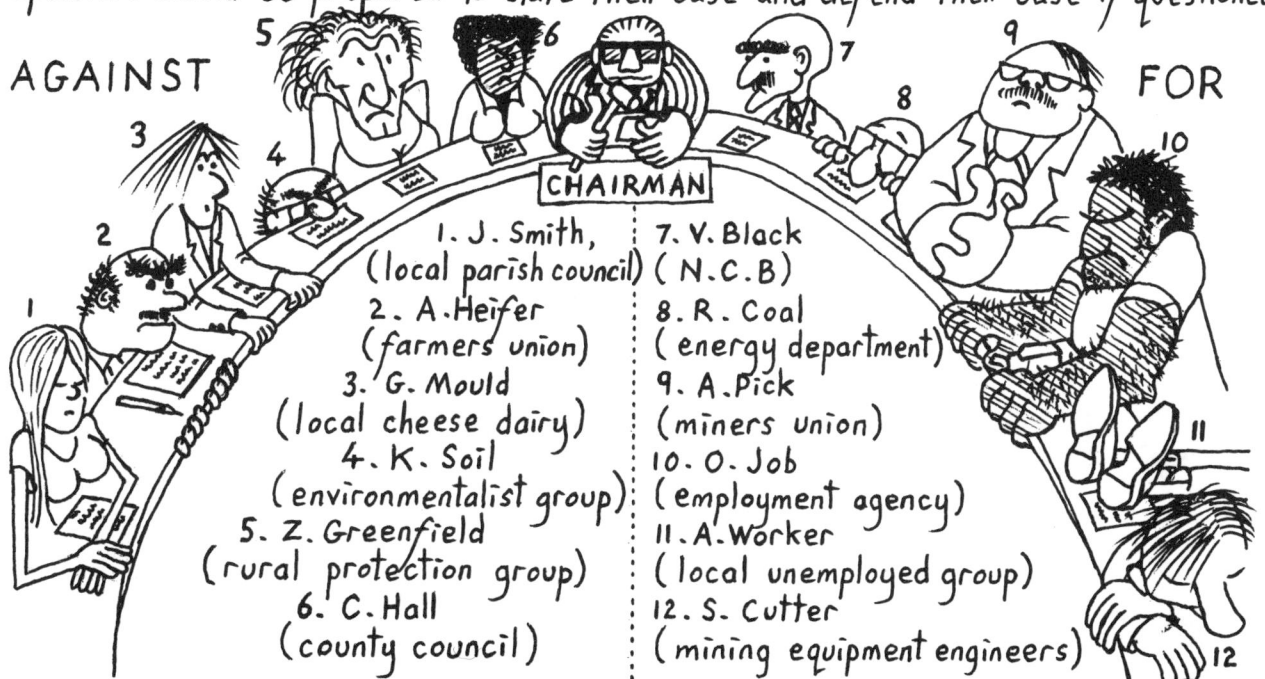

AGAINST   FOR

CHAIRMAN

1. J. Smith,   7. V. Black
(local parish council)   (N.C.B)
2. A. Heifer   8. R. Coal
(farmers union)   (energy department)
3. G. Mould   9. A. Pick
(local cheese dairy)   (miners union)
4. K. Soil   10. O. Job
(environmentalist group)   (employment agency)
5. Z. Greenfield   11. A. Worker
(rural protection group)   (local unemployed group)
6. C. Hall   12. S. Cutter
(county council)   (mining equipment engineers)

STAGE ④ Collect all notes, sketches, photographs, maps and newspaper cuttings to make up a scrap book following the progress of the development.

NOTE: Acknowledgement for this exercise is given on page 84.

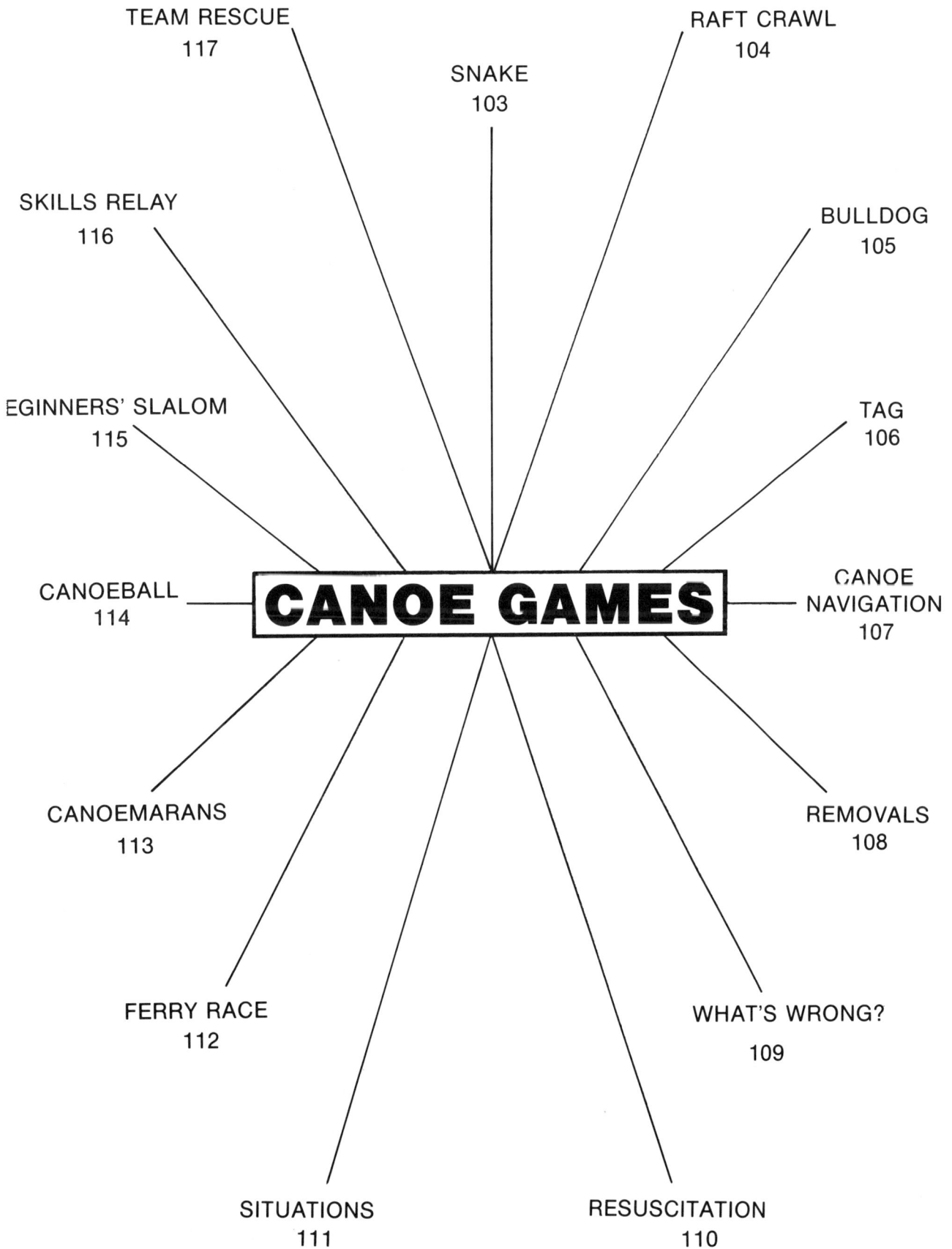

CHAPTER SIX

TEAM RESCUE
117

SNAKE
103

RAFT CRAWL
104

SKILLS RELAY
116

BULLDOG
105

EGINNERS' SLALOM
115

TAG
106

CANOEBALL
114

CANOE GAMES

CANOE
NAVIGATION
107

CANOEMARANS
113

REMOVALS
108

FERRY RACE
112

WHAT'S WRONG?
109

SITUATIONS
111

RESUSCITATION
110

CANOE GAMES

The games and activities in this final chapter have been selected primarily for young beginners' groups. Hopefully they will complement the essential skills training common to all beginners' courses, and provide a little controlled fun in a sport which must be very safety conscious.

I have found that youngsters tend to improve their canoeing skills when they are in a game situation such as 'Tag', 'Bulldog' or 'Canoeball'. The games help to provide motivation, and the newly learned skills are automatically put into operation in the process of chasing after a ball, or avoiding another canoeist in a game of 'Tag'.

There is no substitute however for frequent skills practice sessions with the instructor demonstrating good techniques while the students watch, and then try out the techniques. The instructor is always close at hand to offer correction and guidance. These basic training sessions form the basis for beginners' courses, and are especially important for students who are aiming for the British Canoe Union's tests and certificates. A detailed section entitled 'Notes on Teaching Techniques for Instructors and Coaches' is given in the BCU's Coaching Handbook. This Handbook is hereby acknowledged for its value in compiling this chapter, and for its usefulness over recent years in my teaching.

The pages in this chapter have been arranged so that the easiest games appear towards the beginning, and the more difficult games appear at the end. The chapter starts with a game called "Snake" which could well fit into ten minutes of the first session of a beginners' course. The students are given turns at being the leader, who snakes around in his or her canoe, with the other students trying to follow on. This is done at slow to moderate paddling pace.

Three exercises have been included which could be used for indoor training sessions. These are : 'What's Wrong ?', 'Resuscitation' and 'Situations'. The intention here is that the visual resources may lead to discussion with instructor and students. They could also be used as oral or written assessment exercises if appropriate to the course.

I would consider the 'Team Rescue' exercise to be the most difficult in the chapter, if it is to be done quickly and effectively in a deep water capsize situation.

Finally, I would like to stress the need for strict supervision, and attention to the 'Dos and Don'ts for canoeists' which are given in the Safety chapter of the BCU's Coaching Handbook. Any group leader or teacher intending to use these games should of course be an experienced and qualified canoeist.

SNAKE

RAFT CRAWL

Most canoe instructors would show their students how to 'raft up' the canoes (see sketch below) at an early stage in their course. This method provides stability in open water, and gives the beginners a feeling of security. An interesting development is to have a raft crawl race. Each student in turn climbs out of his or her canoe, crawls along the front of the canoe raft and then along the back of the raft to return to his or her own place. The instructor starts to time each student when satisfied that everyone is holding the raft firmly together.

NOTE: 1) In windy conditions the raft will soon drift away, therefore the instructor would obviously need to be alert for any hazards. 2) The students should realise that the canoes can be easily damaged if anyone attempts to walk or run along the canoe raft.

BULLDOG

To play 'canoe bulldog', one chosen student is positioned in the middle of a river, facing the rest of the group who are lined up along one bank. When the instructor gives the signal to start, the rest of the group try to paddle past the middle student (within set boundaries) to reach the opposite river bank. The middle student aims to touch as many people as possible on the arm or body, with his or her paddle blade. This is done gently! As soon as anyone is touched, then they help to prevent others from passing. The instructor gives the signal for each crossing to start, only when satisfied that everyone is in position. Several crossings may be needed before everyone is touched by a paddle.

SAFETY : Before the game starts, all students should understand that if anyone capsizes, then the others should immediately come to help.

TAG

In this variation of 'tag', the players leave their paddles on the bank side, and only use their hands for propulsion. When one player has been touched, he or she then helps to tag the others. Another alternative which will test the students' balancing skills, is to play the same game with legs hanging outside the canoe.

CANOE NAVIGATION

This exercise is similar to the 'Leading in Turn' exercise in chapter one, in that each student is given responsibility for navigating and leading the group for a given leg of the route. The instructor would need to prepare several large scale waterproof maps with check points circled and numbered. Members of the canoe group would benefit from a practice session in setting a map and setting a compass bearing from a map, before the canoe navigation exercise. The instructor accompanies the canoe group around the course to give guidance and to assess the performance of each student leader.

REMOVALS

The aim of this game is to see which team can transport a given pile of equipment across a lake in the shortest time. Only two teams of two people are allowed to compete at any one time. The equipment to be transported may include items such as canoes, paddles and buoyancy aids from other members of the group. In addition to these items a selection of empty water containers may be used. Equipment should not be carried in the cockpits. An unrestricted exit from the canoe would be needed in the event of a capsize situation.

WHAT'S WRONG?

NATURE RESERVE

PRIVATE WATER NO CANOEING!

DANGER WEIR

CANOE INSTRUCTOR

What should be the correct way?

RESUSCITATION

'Bill, I said practice the Holger Nielson method of artificial respiration, **not** the Half Nelson!'

'Brenda, when I said practice the mouth to mouth method, I did **not** mean kiss him!'

Any canoeist would find some benefit from learning basic first aid techniques. A <u>drowning</u> situation is always a remote possibility, therefore training in artificial resuscitation is a valuable aspect of any canoeing course. Detailed guidelines on artificial resuscitation are given in 'First Aid, The Authorised Manual of St. John Ambulance Association and Brigade', and in the British Canoe Union's Coaching Handbook.

SITUATIONS

① Your friend's canoe hits a rock and starts to sink. You are ten miles from the nearest village, and half way along a fast flowing river in the Scottish Highlands.

④ One member of your canoe group starts to show signs of suffering from hypothermia. You are only three miles from the finish of a twenty mile team race along the River Tees, on a cold December morning.

② A speed boat has just whizzed past your beginners' group in the middle of Lake Windermere. The waves from the boat have caused two children to capsize.

⑤ A group of experienced canoeists have canoed along a stretch of the Yorkshire coast. As they approach their destination they find that there is no easy way into shore. Very large breakers are pounding onto the beach, and a dangerous looking swell is visible at the pier. The only safe landing point is three miles along the coast.

③ Your canoe group drives past an inviting stretch of river which unfortunately is private. Most of the group would like to stop and do some canoeing.

PRIVATE

What would YOU do in these situations ?   Give your reasons.

Note : These situations are intended as discussion points for instructors and students.

FERRY RACE

The aim of this game is to see which team can ferry their passenger across a lake, and return to the same point in the shortest time. A distance of about fifty metres is adequate for each journey. Each team has three people (including one passenger), two canoes, and one paddle. Each team member should change positions at the half way point. The passenger should not stand on the canoes as this could easily cause damage. This game is obviously intended for a warm, sunny day in summer, as the passenger could end up in the water.

SAFETY: Buoyancy aids should be worn by all students.

CANOEMARANS

These makeshift sailing craft are intended <u>only for use on safe, shallow lakes, in light winds</u>.

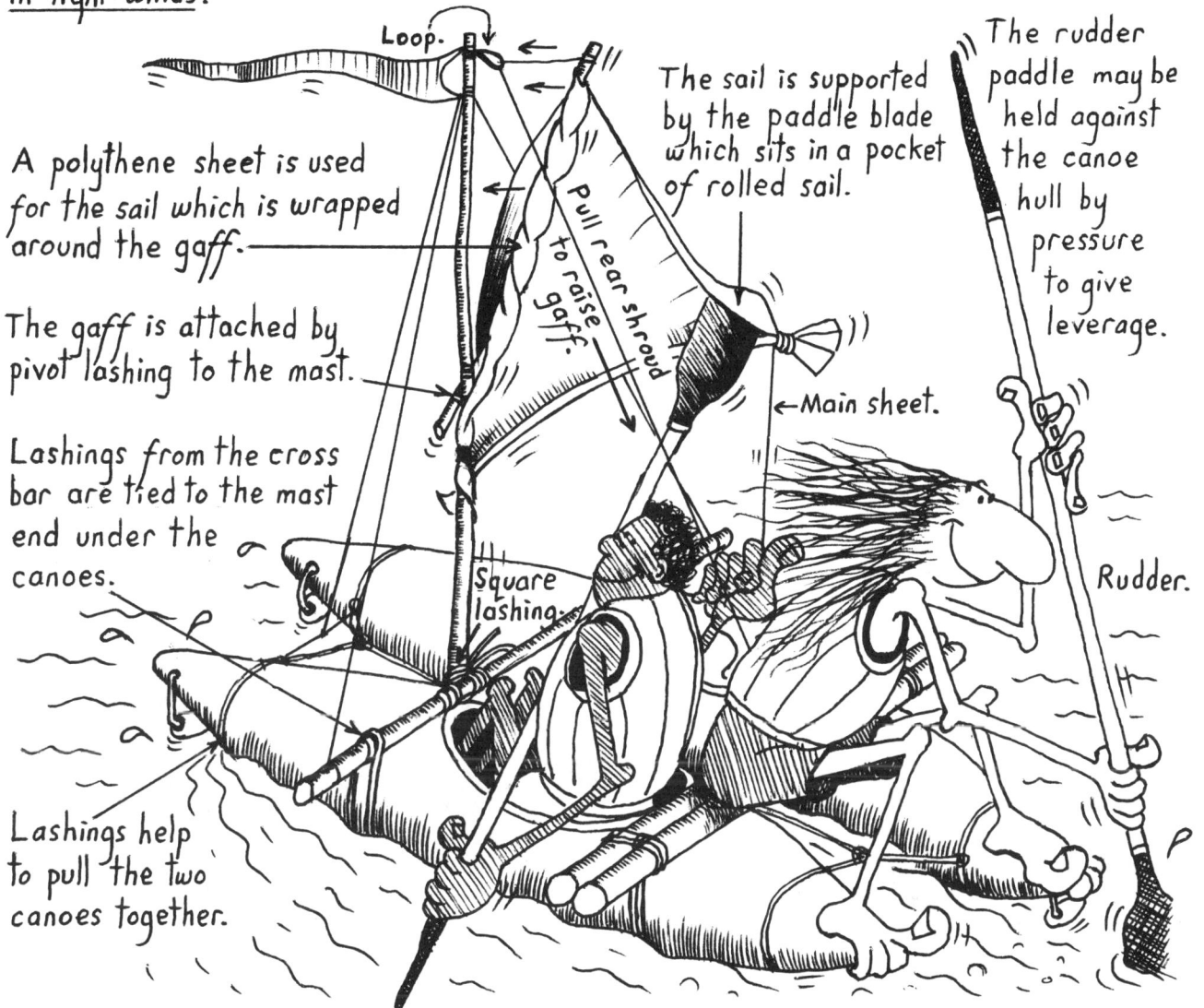

Loop.

The sail is supported by the paddle blade which sits in a pocket of rolled sail.

The rudder paddle may be held against the canoe hull by pressure to give leverage.

A polythene sheet is used for the sail which is wrapped around the gaff.

Pull rear shroud to raise gaff.

The gaff is attached by pivot lashing to the mast.

Lashings from the cross bar are tied to the mast end under the canoes.

←Main sheet.

Rudder.

Square lashing.

Lashings help to pull the two canoes together.

<u>SAFETY POINTS</u>:

1. The instructor should be confident that the canoemarans cannot drift into deep or dangerous areas.

2. All knots and fittings should be checked by the instructor before the craft is carried onto the water.

3. The students should know how to stop the craft, eg by releasing the sail, and by using both paddles as in a normal canoe emergency stop. The students may resort to paddling at any time.

SHARKS!

Don't be tempted to take the canoemarans onto open water or the sea, as I foolishly did on one occasion off the Kintyre peninsula in Scotland. The craft proved to be a successful means of fishing for mackerel, but it failed to manoeuvre properly when we were approached by a large basking shark.

CANOEBALL

The basic idea is that two teams aim to score a goal with a plastic football, by passing (by hand) between members of the team. Goal posts may be improvised on the bank side, or one goal may be used if necessary. A player must not hold the ball for more than three seconds. The paddle may only be used to manoeuvre the canoe, to intercept the ball in the air, or to reach the ball on the water. The referee may award a free throw for infringements of the rules. The ball is thrown in by the non offending team if the ball goes out of the play area.

<u>Note</u>: Players should be penalized for dangerous use of the paddle.
<u>Variations</u>: i) The game can also be played very successfully without paddles; ii) The game may be played without goals, in the middle of a lake or river, although the aim in this case would be for each team to keep possession of the ball for as long as possible, by passing the ball between members of the team.
<u>Value</u>: Fun, confidence in the canoe, manoeuvring skills, team effort, sporting spirit, challenging activity, determination.
<u>Note</u>: This page is based on the very popular game 'Canoe Polo', further details of which are given in the BCU's Coaching Handbook.

BEGINNERS' SLALOM

A beginners' slalom training course can be set up fairly quickly, using long canes or posts which are pushed into the lake or river bed. Some of the problems set on top class slalom courses can also be used on still or slow moving water, offering the beginners a chance to test out their skills in a controlled situation. As in top class competitions, all competitors would be timed with a stop watch.

② Turn and reverse through narrow gate.

① Manoeuvre forwards between narrow gates.

③ Turn and draw stroke across to forward gate.

④ Limbo.

⑤ Throw the paddle over high gate, collect paddle and sprint to the finish line.

SAFETY : Even on a simple training course such as this, there are likely to be many capsizes. All students should therefore have practised the capsize drill before this session.

SKILLS RELAY

This is a useful way of assessing basic canoeing skills towards the end of a beginners' course. Two relay teams line up on the bank with their canoes ready. When the instructor gives the signal to start, the first person in each relay team carries his or her canoe to the water and performs the techniques shown below. The other members of each relay team then follow on in turn, to complete the same techniques. The first relay team to complete all techniques to a satisfactory standard is the winner. The instructor may prefer to use a scoring system so that each technique is awarded points.

① Launching and embarking using a draw stroke.

⑤ Backward paddling.

② 360° turn using a sweep stroke.

⑥ Support stroke on both sides.

(This one didn't work!)

③ Forward paddling.

⑦ Coming alongside and disembarking.

④ Emergency stop.

TEAM RESCUE

When students have progressed beyond the elementary stages of canoeing, they should begin to learn various rescue techniques. The team exercise below shows a very stable method of emptying an upturned kayak in deep water. Notice that the person in the water helps to lift or lower his kayak when required. When the kayak has been emptied, the capsized canoeist may reach across as shown in stage two below, and then quickly slide his feet down into the kayak.

STAGE ① : Rafting together and emptying the kayak over the two hulls.

STAGE ② : Re-entry.

NOTE : A detailed section on deep water rescue techniques is given in the British Canoe Union's Coaching Handbook.

RECOMMENDED BOOKS AND RESOURCES

RECOMMENDED BOOKS

SAFETY IN OUTDOOR PURSUITS   DES Safety Series No 1   H.M.S.O. 1986

FIRST AID MANUAL   St. John Ambulance, St Andrew's Ambulance Association and the British Red Cross   Dorling. Kindersley   1987

THE DUKE OF EDINBURGH AWARD SCHEME EXPEDITION GUIDE   1986

MOUNTAINCRAFT AND LEADERSHIP   Eric Langmuir   British Mountaineering Council   1984

MOUNTAINEERING   Alan Blackshaw   Penguin   new edition due 1988

ORIENTEERING   John Disley   Faber and Faber   1978

YOUR WAY WITH MAP AND COMPASS   John Disley

KNOW THE GAME ORIENTEERING   produced in collaboration with The Scottish Orienteering Association   A and C. Black   1985

MAPMAKING FOR ORIENTEERS   Robin Harvey   British Orienteering Federation

TEACHING ORIENTEERING, A HANDBOOK FOR TEACHERS, INSTRUCTORS AND COACHES   Carol McNeill, Jean Ramsden and Tom Renfrew   Harveys in conjunction with The British Orienteering Federation   1987

SCOUT PIONEERING   John Sweet   The Scouts Association   1986

COACHING HANDBOOK   Geoff Good and Bob Gray   British Canoe Union   currently reprinting

OTHER PUBLICATIONS

ITRC

THE SMALL GROUP HOLIDAY GUIDE   Alan Dearling   Scottish I.T. Resourse Centre

DIRECTORY OF OUTDOOR EDUCATION CENTRES   Sports Council Information Centre

EXPLORING THE ENVIRONMENT   Roger Clare   Macdonald Colour Units

DISCOVERING DERBYSHIRE   Harry Tolley   University of Nottingham School of Education   1982

EYE ON THE ENVIRONMENT   teachers' pack   Council for Environmental Education   1987

SAFETY ON MOUNTAINS   John Jackson   Central Council of Physical Recreation

STONEHENGE   Department of the Environment Official Handbook   R.S. Newall   H.M.S.O.

TRAINING EVENTS FOR ORIENTEERING (O-TECH SHEET No. 1)   Tony Thornley   British Orienteering Federation   1977

OBSERVERS POCKET SERIES   e.g. BIRDS, GRASSES, WILD FLOWERS, TREES, GEOLOGY, POND LIFE, WEATHER

THE FOREST (microcomputer orienteering simulation game) Cunning Running Software

JOURNALS, MAGAZINES and PERIODICALS

FOOTLOOSE   monthly

HIGH   monthly

MOUNTAIN   bimonthly

CLIMBER and RAMBLER   monthly

GREAT OUTDOORS   monthly

COUNTRY WALKING   bimonthly

COMPASS SPORT   bimonthly

CANOE FOCUS   bimonthly   available through the B.C.U.

BBC WILDLIFE   monthly

TEACHING GEOGRAPHY   quarterly   available through the Geographical Assoc.

ORGANISATIONS

BRITISH ORIENTEERING FEDERATION   'Riversdale', Dale Road North, Darley Dale, Matlock, Derbyshire DE4 2HX

YOUTH HOSTELS ASSOCIATION (England and Wales)   Trevelyan House, 8 St. Stephen's Hill, St. Albans, Herts. AL1 2DY

YOUTH HOSTELS ASSOCIATION (Scotland)   7 Glebe Crescent, Stirling FR8 2JA

THE SCOUT ASSOCIATION   Baden-Powell House, Queen's Gate, London SW7 5JS

BRITISH CANOE UNION   Flexel House, 45/47 High Street, Addlestone, Weybridge, Surrey KT15 1JV

SPORTS COUNCIL INFORMATION CENTRE   70 Brompton Road, London SW3 1EX

COUNCIL FOR ENVIRONMENTAL EDUCATION   School of Education, University of Reading, London Road, Reading RG1 5AQ

ORDNANCE SURVEY   Romsey Road, Maybush, Southampton SO9 4DH

THE WATCH TRUST FOR ENVIRONMENTAL EDUCATION   22 The Green, Nettleham, Lincoln LN2 2NR

ROYAL SOCIETY FOR THE PROTECTION OF BIRDS   The Lodge, Sandy, Bedfordshire

THE MOUNTAIN WALKING LEADER TRAINING BOARD   Crawford House, Precinct Centre, Booth Street East, Manchester M13 9RZ

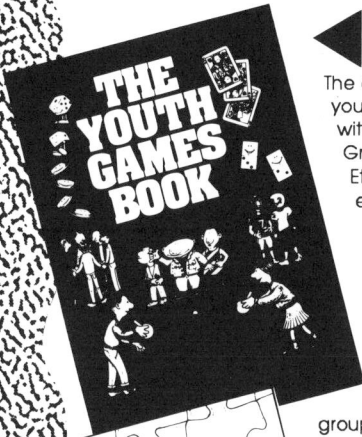

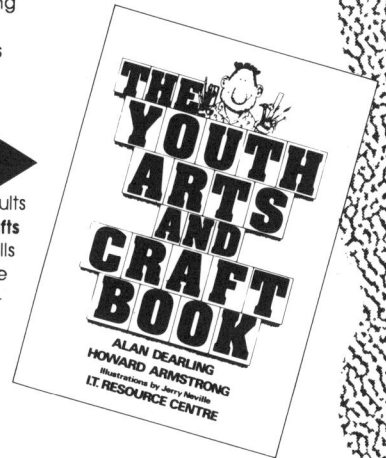

NOTES

NOTES

NOTES